Contents

Acknowledgments

This book is part of the Politics of Patents (POP) project that has received funding from the European Research Council (ERC) under the European Union's Horizon 2020 research and innovation program, Grant No. 819458.

Kat, Ellen, Katja, and Nikki are very grateful to all the designers in this book for their generosity and enthusiasm for this project. In particular, we thank Sky Cubacub, founder of *Rebirth Garments*, for permission to use the fabulous image on the cover. We also extend heartfelt thanks to all the people involved in the POP project and, more broadly, friends and colleagues throughout the sociology department of Goldsmiths College, who supported this research at different stages over the years: Paul Stoneman, Claudia Di Gianfrancesco, Katalin Halász, Adele Mason-Bertrand, Rebecca Coleman, Michaela Benson, Melissa Nolas, Evelyn Rupert, Dan Neyland, and Chloe Nast. We also greatly appreciated the feedback and constructive comments from the anonymous reviewers who helped to shape this final manuscript.

Front cover credit: Rebirth Garments, Colectivo Multipolar, and Sky Cubacub / Model: Sky Cubacub

Introduction: Wearable World-Making

EMBODIED ACTS OF RESISTANCE

Desire lines are informal tracks trodden or cycled into dirt and grass over time. They can be shortcuts or long meanderings that slice across parks and wind around obstacles. Found in cultures and societies worldwide, desire lines make a striking contrast to networks of roads and paths made of tar and stone. The latter are formal systems that shape (and are shaped by) normative and normalizing experiences of the world. Desire lines do something else. Feminist and queer scholar Sara Ahmed writes about how desire lines map "where people deviate from the paths they are supposed to follow."[1] Some call them "free-will ways"[2] while others view them as records of "civil disobedience."[3] These cumulative mappings show how individuals use their bodies to shape the worlds they live in. In the process, they provide clear evidence of how "the built environment doesn't always fit the needs of the people it's meant to serve."[4] In these ways, desire lines can be seen as everyday embodied acts of resistance and world-making.

This book is about the designers of desire lines. It is about individuals forging collective tracks and traces between and around dominant official practices in order to see, explore, and experiment with the practices and politics that signify and enable other ways of living. In the following interviews, twenty-six designers reveal how they imagine, invent, and inhabit new worlds beyond conventional norms. While their focuses and motivations vary, all recognize the needs of diverse groups—for example, asylum-seeker and transgender communities—who are commonly ignored, underresourced, or actively discriminated against by current dominant cultural practices. These designers take ordinary things and invest them with extraordinary meanings and inspiring possibilities. Their primary tool of change? Wearables.

THE EXTRAORDINARINESS OF ORDINARY THINGS

Wearables can be most simply defined as "things that can be worn." In contrast to the widespread and popular notion of "wearable technologies," the term "wearables" isn't restricted to referring only to "high-tech" and "smart" electronic and digital devices (such as watches and fitness trackers). Indeed, wearables aren't limited only to clothing. In this collection, we employ the term "wearable" to include various things worn on bodies: shoes, coats, underwear, stand-up urination devices, prosthetics, and even makeup. While we appreciate how they're made and how they look, we are most interested in what they do: What social, political, or environmental problems are the designers in this collection addressing? How are they attempting to resist, subvert, or disrupt normative conventions built into everyday life? What kinds of conversations do they want to start? Returning to the analogy of desire lines, we want to know: can wearables create possibilities to act differently and what kinds of new worlds might they make?

In his classic book *Cruising Utopia* (published in 2009), queer theorist José Esteban Muñoz[5] encouraged readers to refuse to settle for the status quo. He argued that "we must dream and enact new and better pleasures; other ways of being in the world, and ultimately new worlds." His hopeful text rejects the flat, routinized, heteronormative structures of the privileged few and instead calls for colorful reimaginings of expansive and diverse futures. This is why our book is called *Wearable Utopias*; the ubiquity of wearables, their proximity to the body, and transformative potential make them a potent platform for catalyzing new worlds. We hope the chorus of creative voices in the pages that follow reveal not only glimpses of other, more expansive worlds, but also ways of interrupting and inhabiting existing ones.

Our approach to the twenty-three interviews that follow is framed by science and technology studies (STS), feminist technoscience, and cultural and gender studies. What we choose—or are compelled—to wear has long been central to the forces of belonging, identity, protest, power, and discrimination. We're interested in how wearables render visible critical social and civic issues, raise new questions about taken-for-granted ideas, and assist people whose claims for freedoms, rights, and recognition have been ignored by conventional worldviews. We take wearables seriously as artifacts of "nonverbal resistance"[6] and "public struggle and contestation" and draw attention to how they serve "to enact distinctive ideals of citizenship and participation."[7] This requires paying close attention to the role of *things* in the making of worlds. As technofeminist Donna Haraway reminds us, "It matters what matters we use to think other matters with; it matters what stories we tell to tell other stories with . . . it matters what stories make worlds, what worlds make stories."[8] And things, as sociologist Bruno Latour explains in *Making Things Public*, are central to the making of an "object-oriented democracy."

> Each object gathers around itself a different assembly of relevant parties. Each object triggers new occasions to passionately different and dispute. Each object may also offer new ways of achieving closure without having to agree. In other words, objects—taken as so many issues—bind us all in ways that map out a public space profoundly different from what is usually recognised under the label of "the political."[9]

Wearables are such things—critical sites and tools of sociopolitical power, gender relations, and world-making—and they touch every single human body on the planet. Anthropologist Daniel Miller wrote in a provocatively titled piece "Why Clothing is not Superficial" that the things we wear "are among our most personal possessions" and "the main medium between our sense of our bodies and our sense of the external world."[10] Yet despite their ubiquity, clothes have long been overlooked as being merely decorative or boringly practical. It's a view that diminishes their role as easily accessible potential sites of radical action. "It is true that, in times of crisis, what we wear can feel like the most trivial of concerns," writes academic and critic Shahidha Bari, yet "isn't it curious that so many of our most heated cultural disputes should circle around the right to wear particular clothes in particular circumstances."[11] Fortunately, the early decades of the twenty-first century have seen increased recognition of the social significance not only of wearables but also of wearable designers in cultural life, political discourse, and global creative industries.[12]

Paying attention to the extraordinariness of ordinary things is a research technique familiar to STS scholars. From sewers and seatbelts to dog-leads and bicycles, studying taken-for-granted things that service everyday life can reveal how people navigate and make sense of the worlds around them.[13] Susan Leigh Star has advocated for the study of "boring" things.[14] Latour called attention to the "missing masses"[15] and Mike Michael argues that everyday things "contribute to, and disrupt, the unnoticed, everyday, and always present co(a)gents that populate our world."[16] A focus on wearables—as a mundane yet essential technoscience of everyday life—can reveal what people value, rely upon, or use in unexpected ways to work around problems or address restrictions or limitations. In some cases, wearables can become vehicles for journeys that might be entirely different from those that were originally intended.

Of course, what is considered mundane or ordinary can radically differ between citizens. It can signal an "unmarked and unrecognised way of being in the world" that privileges some bodies over others.[17] "Misfits," explains leading disability studies scholar Rosemarie Garland-Thomson, emerge "when the environment does not sustain the shape and function of the body that enters it."[18] Using the analogy of trying to fit a square peg into a round hole, she advocates for changing the hole, not the peg. She argues that "social justice and equal access should be achieved by changing the shape of the world, not changing the shape of our bodies."[19] In this context, *misfitting* is not something that needs to be fixed by changing the individual; rather, worlds should be made to be more flexible, diverse, and open. This perspective powerfully reframes assumptions tied to specific bodies by "highlighting adaptability, resourcefulness, and subjugated knowledge as potential effects of misfitting." Throughout the book, we closely attend to designers' experiences and creative responses to contexts and experiences where people and things don't fit. Their situated knowledge, as Haraway argues, shapes what is possible to know and "allows us to become answerable for what we learn how to see."[20]

This book also pays attention to use, misuse, and what Ahmed calls "queer use." She writes about how "when we use something in ways that were not intended, we are allowing those qualities to acquire freer expression."[21] There is much evidence of extraordinary uses of ordinary wearables throughout history. Art historian Rosika Parker has argued that "the art of embroidery has been the means of educating women into the feminine ideal, and of proving that they have attained it, but it has also provided a weapon of resistance to the constraints of femininity."[22] Parker is writing about how, for centuries, women have used all the tools, skills, and networks at their disposal—especially at times when they lacked access to normative legal instruments to claim their rights. Through wearables (and practices related to wearables), they redefined the parameters of their freedoms, pushed at the boundaries of conventionality, and renegotiated what might be possible. Small, seemingly ordinary actions can reveal how people gain a political voice and how citizens are made, as well as how different worlds are imagined, invented, and inhabited.

THE ROLE OF WEARABLES IN CIVIC CONCERNS

Citizenship reveals a great deal about society, in terms of what kinds of beliefs, practices, and people are recognized, rewarded, or rejected. Being a citizen, as per historian and philosopher Hannah Arendt, includes having "the right to have rights."[23] Yet, as Arendt and others have argued, it is far from straightforward and fixed. According to feminist theorist Ruth Lister, it has always been "an essentially contested concept."[24] Discussions of who has citizenship, who deserves it, and who can be stripped of it dominate public discourse worldwide. Accounts of people fleeing devastating persecution, global warming, disasters, pollution, and war fill our screens daily. Even those who are permitted citizenship—such as women, working-class people, and those with impairments—do not always have equal access to rights due to other systemic inequalities.[25] Disability scholar Marie Sépulchre argues that "formal equal citizenship rights do not necessarily mean equal possibilities to enjoy rights in reality because people have unequal access to socio-material resources."[26] To help those in need, many people house refugees, donate money and goods, volunteer and take to the streets in protest. Critical citizenship scholars who study these kinds of ground-up actions argue that citizenship is not just about access to information, legal status, passports, or relations with the nation-state. It is also something that is practiced, negotiated, claimed, performed, struggled for, and made material in everyday mundane contexts.[27]

Political scholars Engin Isin and Greg Neilson explain that "acts of citizenship" draw attention away from formal systems and institutions to "collective or individual deeds that rupture social-historical patterns."[28] It is a concept that shifts "from what people *say* (opinion, perception, attitudinal surveys) to what people *do*."[29] This expanded approach to citizenship studies reveals how people use creative means to make claims to rights and entitlements that would otherwise be unavailable to them. In the process, they express new forms of civic engagement and participation.[30] Sometimes, as Paula Hildebrandt and Sybille Peters argue, "to perform citizenship and to act as citizen includes a certain dimension of 'fake it 'til you make it.'"[31] As such, alternative acts and performances of citizenship don't have to be large scale, radically subversive, or even overtly obvious to outsiders to have an impact. What they offer individuals is a means to participate, feel recognized, engage with, contribute to, and otherwise shape social and political worlds around them. In other words, they offer a way of "doing rights with things" rather than doing things with rights.[32]

In our larger European Research Council–funded research project Politics of Patents (abbreviated to POP),[33] we examine how inventors throughout the past two hundred years have used wearables, evidenced via patents, to reimagine how citizens resist, negotiate, or remake claims to civic rights and public life. Extending this line of thought, in this book, we are interested in how contemporary wearables might be viewed as alternative forms of material participation and political engagement. Sociologist Noortje Marres explains how "letting things in" to analysis marks a shift from knowledge-based framings of citizenship to more object-oriented versions. She argues that a shift toward analyses of objects can deepen the "understanding of democracy and public action as they focus attention on the capacities of things to facilitate, inform and organize citizenship and engagement."[34] Similarly, in design research,

Carl Disalvo argues that the study of things can reveal "how our worlds are configured, and how they might be configured differently."[35]

This is central to our aim in *Wearable Utopias*. We explore things in the form of wearable acts of resistance and performances of citizenship. These include, for example, the ability to move freely, be heard, feel safe, access resources, and assert other equal rights otherwise denied or limited. To locate such things, we combine several fields of design to find designers who share the aim of inventing new civic and social realities from the ground up using an array of resources, skills, and materials. Through the interviews that follow, we explore ordinary wearables as extraordinary sites of personal expression, public engagement, and political action. Like other scholars committed to understanding the potential of everyday material participation in amplifying political life, we search for "mundane, everyday 'low-tech' artefacts and their ability to generate or reinforce novel forms of citizenship."[36] As Isin and Neilson remind us, "Acts of citizenship create a sense of the possible and of citizenship that is 'yet to come.'"[37]

A COLLECTION OF CREATIVE CONVERSATIONS

Wearable Utopias features contributions from artists, architects, activists, makers, designers, and teachers. They are workwear and technical practitioners, underwear and accessories designers, streetwear and activewear experts, and industrialwear and adaptivewear professionals. They are new graduates and experienced business owners, specialist technicians and researchers, who work individually or in teams, with interdisciplinary collaborators or community groups. Their ages span from early twenties to mid-seventies, and they hail from around the globe.

Interviews in this collection were conducted online when COVID-19 lockdowns were sweeping the world. We have minimized our voices as interviewers so as to amplify those of our interlocutors, retaining the informal interview-style format for its liveliness and dynamism. Our voices as editors become more evident in the introductions to each chapter and the book's conclusion. In these sections, we frame contributions in relation to the key questions indicated above and briefly point to critical writings about these subjects. As such, each chapter offers theoretical, conceptual, and material practice-based insights for radical thinking with, about, and in wearable form. We include links in each interview for those curious to learn more.

As editors, we have tried to amass a collection that is culturally, geographically, and gender diverse so as to spark conversations and questions about a range of civic and social issues. There are many more ideas and interviews that we've not been able to include. (We talked with fifty different designers in total and only a portion are featured here.) With regard to this collection, we are aware of and continually reflect on our own positionalities as white, cisgender, able-bodied researchers located in London, United Kingdom, with access to significant social, cultural, and financial capital. Here we harness our privileges to share and showcase the work of others who are bravely imagining, inventing, and inhabiting new worlds. Another way we are doing this is by directing all profits from this publication to not-for-profit organizations agreed on with the contributors to further support their important work.

ORGANIZATION OF THE BOOK

Wearable Utopias is organized along six social and political themes that shape citizens' abilities to participate in public life: expanding, moving, concealing, connecting, leaking, and working.

Chapter 1—Expanding opens the book by locating wearables in public space and discussing why this matters for citizenship. It focuses on wearables that draw attention to physical, social, and political boundaries that empower some citizens while limiting others. The designers in this chapter recognize the ways in which many groups—people with different body shapes, transgender and gender-diverse people, immigrants, and those with impairments—can be reduced, silenced, overlooked, or actively erased from public space, visual culture, and civic life. Their responses creatively expand possibilities for a diverse range of citizens to occupy more or different spaces, become visible, and engage with or renegotiate everyday experiences. This chapter features interviews with Sky Cubacub (*Rebirth Garments*), Karoline Vitto (*Body as Material*), Robin Lasser and Adrienne Pao (*Dress Tents*), and

Dani Clode (*Third Thumb*, *Vine Arm*, *Materialise Arm*, and *Synchronised Arm*).

Being able to lead an active life shapes health and well-being, a sense of freedom, and ideas about civic participation. In Chapter 2—Moving, we focus on wearables designed to enable sporting and active lifestyles. These interviews cover modest activewear for girls and women, antiharassment cyclewear, and DIY patterns for everyday activewear. We also discuss social distancing challenges arising from COVID-19 and how one designer used wearables to invite citizens back into public space and to encourage interactions between strangers. This chapter features interviews with Aheda Zanetti (*Burqini*), Melissa Fehr (*Fehr Trade*), Ester van Kempen (*Ride With Wolves*), and Nicolas Moser (*Petticoat Dress* and *Urban Blanket*).

In Chapter 3—Concealing, we talk to designers who develop wearables to defend privacy or help people keep secrets. We explore anti-surveillance coats to protect wearers' data, protest communication kits for high-intensity policing situations, and a distinctive use of makeup to camouflage the face from facial recognition technology. We also hear from a designer who hacks cisnormative styles to tailor wearables to suit nonbinary wearers. Rendering things visible can draw critical attention to an issue, as in the case of surveillance systems. However, certain citizens already garner too much attention of the sort that leaves them vulnerable to discrimination and violence. All the designers raise and reflect on the tensions of sociopolitical in/visibility. This chapter features interviews with Leon Baauw (*Project KOVR*), Pedro Oliveira and Xuedi Chen (*Backslash*), Sissel Kärneskog (*I am THEM*), and Emily Roderick and Georgina Rowlands (*The Dazzle Club*).

Most wearables are worn on individual bodies. Yet how they are designed, made, and understood is always a collective process. Chapter 4—Connecting explores the use of wearables in linking communities across bodies, time, and space. Here designs play a key role in bringing people together to challenge social and political narratives and to involve them in addressing large-scale issues. We learn about a knitted hat that connected millions of people to forge a powerful political moment and how a simple pair of jeans worn en masse could address the urgent issue of air pollution. This chapter also includes inspiring accounts of diverse cultural communities sharing stories, experiences, and skills through radical acts of joy. This chapter features interviews with Krista Suh (*Pussyhat Project*), Dewi Cooke (*The Social Studio*), Helen Storey (*Catalytic Clothing*), and Lucy Orta (*Refuge Wear* and *Nexus Architecture*).

The focus of Chapter 5—Leaking explores the stigma associated with "leaking bodies" that too frequently prevents citizens from being able to fully participate in many aspects of public life. For example, some people's freedoms—especially women, gender-diverse people, people who are unhoused, and disabled people—can be limited by inadequate or unequal facilities in the form of toilets in social, retail, and work spaces. These inequalities foster the pervasive notion that some public places are not for everyone. Designers in this chapter challenge the idea that leaking bodies are problematic or taboo by viewing these kinds of critical personal needs as catalysts for inventiveness. Their responses take a range of forms: from stand-up urination devices to a washable pocket for sanitary items, and an art practice dedicated to eradicating the shame around menstruation. This chapter includes interviews with Samantha Fountain (*Shewee*), Amelia Kociolkowska (*Carrie*), and Romina Chuls (*Qué Rico Menstruo*).

The workplace and the act of working should be primary sites for the expression of independence and identity. Chapter 6—Working explores how designers respond to work experiences, where privileges and provisions are unequally distributed. They discuss some of the struggles people face across a range of vocations to secure equipment and find professional clothing that fits. This chapter also reflects on gendered histories of workers through stories about Nigerian indigo dyers and how one designer draws on her inspiring entrepreneurial foremothers to design vibrant wearables that emphasize the strength and resilence of women's bodies. We finish with an interview about the possibilities of aging, not only with style but with vitality and joy. This chapter includes interviews with Victoria Jenkins (*Unhidden*), Abiola Onabulé (*Iyá Àlàro*), Mimosa Schmidt (*SÜK*), and Debra Rapoport (*Advanced Style*).

In the concluding chapter, we map ideas emerging across all of the interviews in relation to the core themes of citizenship and world-making, via wearables. We argue that a focus on wearables reveals insights into a range of concerns and controversies that some parts of society live with on a daily basis. It provides alternative perspectives on how experiences of different citizens are "shaped, modified and narrated in order to claim certain rights."[38] We discuss how designers view conventional and narrow binaries as catalysts for inventiveness and the unmaking and redoing of normative understandings. We reflect on emerging forms and practices of citizenship that value multiplicity, flexibility, and diversity. In these ways, this book is permeated with desire lines.

Desire lines press their way into obdurate landscapes. They might initially have minimal impact, but over time and with support, they deepen. Citizens on similar journeys reinforce these paths until they become stable, more easily found, and traversed. In some circumstances, as an alternative path eventually becomes a mainstream route, informal desire lines can turn into formal roads. What might seem to be a lonely individual divergence from the norm can soon become collective and widespread behavior. As Sara Ahmed reminds us, "The hope of changing directions is that we don't always know where some paths may take us" yet it is the "risking departure from the straight and narrow" that "makes futures possible."[39]

1 EXPANDING

The freedom to experience, assemble in, and move through public space has long been considered central to core ideas around citizenship and is codified in laws around the world.[1] The public sphere "is where citizenship is enacted and in which democratic intercourse among citizens occurs."[2] Whether for socializing, work, or protest, public spaces are central to processes of cultural exchange and social cohesion, offering the potential for encounters, collective participation, and action. The idea of having the "right to the city," as penned in 1968 by Henry Lefebvre,[3] involves not only the freedom to interact and participate but also having access to resources. However, it has never been the case that all people have equal capacity to take up or expand into public space. Some fit, while others, to borrow Garland-Thomson's term, misfit.

Compared to the most privileged, some, such as women, children, immigrants, Black people, ethnic minorities, people seeking asylum, Indigenous people, young and aged people, nonbinary people, and people with impairments can have markedly different experiences in public spaces. Far from being able to claim, enjoy, or expand into public space, they are more likely to be ignored, silenced, erased, or outright attacked and persecuted. As Garland-Thomson writes, "The primary negative effect of misfitting is exclusion from the public sphere—a literal casting out—and the resulting segregation into domestic spaces or sheltered institutions."[4] Around the world, the same groups of people are often disproportionally sexualized, surveilled or harassed while simultaneously being underrepresented and undervalued by conservative systems and policies.

Some of these issues derive from the social shaping of public space. As feminist geographer Jane Darke argues, "Any settlement is an inscription in space of the social relations in the society that built it" and many "cities are patriarchy written in stone, brick, glass and concrete."[5] For some, simply being outside sanctioned spaces is to be subjected to unwanted attention and the threat of violence. Geographer Prerna Siwach is among many who critique the "patriarchal bargaining" that shapes who can and cannot inhabit public spaces and whose actions compress and reduce others.[6] For example, women are often socialized to expect that they will not be safe in deserted streets and poorly lit parks, particularly late at night or early in the morning. The expectation is that women should therefore avoid these places in order to preserve their safety rather than for men to refrain from the behaviors that make these places unsafe (or perceived to be unsafe). As feminist scholar Leslie Kern writes, "We can see that the freedom offered to women by contemporary city life is still bound by gendered norms about the proper spaces and roles of women in the city."[7] Challenging these kinds of accepted views and assumptions can be difficult, dangerous or even impossible.

Geographer Doreen Massey and sociologist Nirmal Puwar both vividly capture the experience of feeling "out of place." They explain how a "space invader" is someone who might be able to enter a space but may never feel comfortable, welcome, or accepted within it. As an illustration of this, Massey reflects on the maleness of the football fields in the city where she grew up and how, as a girl, they "seemed barred, another world" to someone like her.[8] Puwar writes, "Some bodies are deemed as having the right to belong, while others are marked out as trespassers, who are, in accordance with how both space and bodies are imagined (politically, historically and conceptually), circumscribed as being 'out of place.'"[9]

Urban planner Eva Kail leads Vienna's gender-sensitive planning approach, established in 1992, to challenge the idea that public space should only cater to one type of citizen—the single, cisgender, able-bodied working man. She writes that "to be able to be in the city, in the way you want to be, shows in a really clear way what your chances in society are." Even more astutely, she notes that "if you are using public space, you are also becoming a public person."[10] The freedom to access and experience shared space and resources comes with the promise of participation, spectatorship, serendipitous encounters, and social and political membership. It is a clear marker of civic participation, with all the rights this entails.

In some contexts, the courage required to "space invade" and claim equal citizenship rights and freedoms cannot be overstated. In 2022, widespread protests by women in Iran, catalyzed by the death of Mahsa (Zhina) Amini after she was taken into custody by "morality police" for improperly wearing her hijab in public space, were met with unprecedented state violence.[11] In India, thousands of people have taken to the streets to protest the sexual harassment and rape of women in public places such as parks and buses.[12] The George Floyd protests, which started in 2020 in Minneapolis, United States, spread around the world, mobilizing millions into the Black Lives Matter[13] movement against police brutality and systemic racism. There are ongoing accounts of violent attacks on LGBTQIA+ people just for being in, and moving through, spaces like public toilets, airports, and libraries. These are just some of the recent ways citizens around the world struggle to equalize the distribution of rights and entitlements. Their experiences demonstrate how public spaces are far from neutral, or as Puwar reminds us, they "are not blank and open for anybody to occupy."[14]

This chapter explores the widespread issues and challenges experienced by some people as they attempt to claim a fuller experience of citizenship in public space. We look for material tactics for expanding into physical, social, and political worlds seemingly off limits to some people. The following designers draw attention to and challenge the idea of who gets to be a public person—a citizen—through wearables. Here wearables are put to use to recognize and value different bodies, liberate ideas, and generate fresh social and political possibilities. In the process, they make or take space, reconfiguring and expanding wearers' lives in the process.

We start the interviews with *Rebirth Garments*, a wearables and accessories line that caters to queer, transgender, and disabled people of all ages and body sizes. Founder and designer **Sky Cubacub** provides accessible and comfortable designs that help commonly ignored or overlooked people to become "radically visible." They explain how their aim is about "taking up space" in visual, sonic, and dynamic ways. Instead of a typical catwalk, Sky invites people with marginalized identities to "claim their bodies" in their "dream outfit." Sky's designs challenge narrow and normative gender binaries by making accessible clothing that is "also exciting and cute and fun and sexy and bright and joyous." Fundamentally, their designs cater for and celebrate the kinds of bodies "that society typically shuns." They "refuse to assimilate" and aim instead to create a "QueerCrip dress reform movement."[15]

Womenswear designer **Karoline Vitto** also draws attention to bodies hidden by society through *Body as Material*. In contrast to clothes that bind and constrict bodies into formulaic shapes (such as conventional hourglass figures), Karoline's mixed-media designs accentuate the beauty of larger bodies. She celebrates their folds, rolls, and curves, and her designs invite wearers to expand their bodies into the world. Her clothes are bought by people who want to "show their bodies, and not to hide them." Karoline explains, "I'm a firm believer that the more you see something, the more you're going to get used to it, and the more you're going to find it beautiful." Through Karoline's wearables, visibility maps onto the politics of representation.

Robin Lasser and **Adrienne Pao** take up the challenge of expanding alternative ideas into public space using a range of large-scale architectural tents in the shape of skirts and dresses. These installations, called *Dress Tents*, are designed to take up physical space as well as intervene in social and political discourse in significant locations worldwide. *Dress Tents* make humorous and captivating spectacles that pull viewers in close and entice them to question important and sometimes uncomfortable ideas. As Robin explains, "There's a sense of a play, wonder, magic . . . a kind of upbeat way of looking at topics that sometimes we choose to turn away from." For Adrienne, the aim of these large-scale wearable installations is "to amplify voices in our society" and "provide space for everybody as best we can."

The final interview is with **Dani Clode**, an augmentation designer who works with neuroscientists, body confidence advocates, and disability activists to challenge the "perspective of what a 'regular' body is." She shares insights into her augmented research projects, *Third Thumb*, *Vine Arm*, *Materialise Arm*, and *Synchronised Arm*. These projects expand the edges of human bodies: "We're exploring how the brain responds to a completely new body part." Dani works closely with interdisciplinary collaborators to explore what it might mean to reimagine the body: "We're at a point now where we can start to think beyond the body . . . we're not restricted by trying to re-create how the body is currently designed." Her designs celebrate the body in all its possible permutations.

Collectively, these designers resist normative compressions, limitations, and restrictions. They refuse conventional labels and assumptions and instead make wearables for a diverse range of bodies, uses, and contexts. In the process, they embrace gender diversity, body positivity, and disability using humor, color, scale, and creativity. The distinctiveness of their contributions lies not only in how their wearables raise the profile and value of distinct social groups within mainstream awareness but also in how they question assumed privileges and social norms. Together, they reveal the expansive possibilities of what happens when a wider variety of people design for a wider variety of people.

Rebirth Garments

Sky Cubacub (they/them/their and xe/xem/xyr)

Chicago, United States
http://rebirthgarments.com

Sky Cubacub [pronounced Koo-Bah-Koob] is the founder of a wearables and accessories line called *Rebirth Garments* and the author of *Radical Visibility: A QueerCrip Dress Reform Movement Manifesto*. They are a nonbinary xenogender and disabled Filipinx queer who designs wearables and accessories for queer, trans, and disabled people of all sizes and ages. Sky's remarkable and expansive creative practice reflects their desire to advocate for those who have often been excluded by mainstream fashion. Their strikingly vibrant and colorful designs challenge conventional beauty standards by expanding ideas around bodies and identities and the possibilities of clothes for personal and political expression.

Can you start by telling us how your creative practice with wearables began?
I started the clothing line in 2014. I had dreamt about it since I was in high school. I started making intricate garments early on, typically from scale-maille and chainmaille.[16]

I was making tons of garments that were super heavy, intricate, repetitive task-type things. I tended to make clothing that didn't quite cover my body much, or at least would cover the parts of my body that were supposed to be covered for high school.

I looked around for unitards and things like that, but they were all either in a black or a pink or a white or just a beige that was supposed to be a nude, but it doesn't go with anybody's skin color. I decided to start making my own, and I learned from my best friends' mom, who is a dancer and a seamstress. She was making lots of unitards in the '80s when she couldn't find things that she liked. She taught me how to use a serger [overlocker] and make spandex clothing. I got really interested in that, but it was still just something to go underneath the clothing that I was already making.

Then, in college, I got more interested in working with the spandex and making intricate garments out of it. But I had to take time off because I got really sick. My stomach stopped working when I was twenty-one and I wasn't able to eat for many months. I still don't have a normal, typical stomach,

Figure 1.1

Credit: *Rebirth Garments* / Model: Sky Cubacub / Photo: *Colectivo Multipolar*

but everything that I put on really hurt me because I used to wear lots of tight skinny jeans and stuff like that. Basically, I stopped being able to wear what I like to call hard pants, like jeans and woven fabric that isn't stretchy. I started making really soft, stretchy clothing for myself.

What were some of the first designs you made?
I had been wanting to make gender-affirming undergarments for trans folks, but, specifically, because I am nonbinary, I was really interested in making something that showed off my identity more. Other gender-affirming undergarments I had seen were just very blah and boring and trying to blend in or just not be seen.

I started thinking about making gender-affirming undergarments when I was at high school. This was not just because the styling of existing garments was unexciting to me, but because I had no access to purchasing those types of garments. They are typically only sold in stores like sex toy shops, at least in the US, and you are not allowed to go into those stores if you are under eighteen and I had no digital money.

I wanted to make something that would be accessible, but also exciting and cute and fun and sexy and bright and joyous. I wanted to make it so that I was comfortable and it went with the disabilities that I was having.

I wanted to make something that would be accessible, but also exciting and cute and fun and sexy and bright and joyous.

Originally, I thought that there were going to be two separate clothing lines: one that was just undergarments or lingerie for trans folks and another that was going to be for people who were disabled, but then, basically, immediately I thought, "No, they should just be the same." I hadn't seen a clothing line that was that intersectional. I know a lot of other people who fall in those identities, and I just thought that type of representation would be really cool.

What are gender-affirming undergarments and who are they for?
Gender-affirming undergarments or underwear are an underlayer that helps you feel what you feel on the inside is echoed on the outside. You want your body to match the identity that you have in your brain.

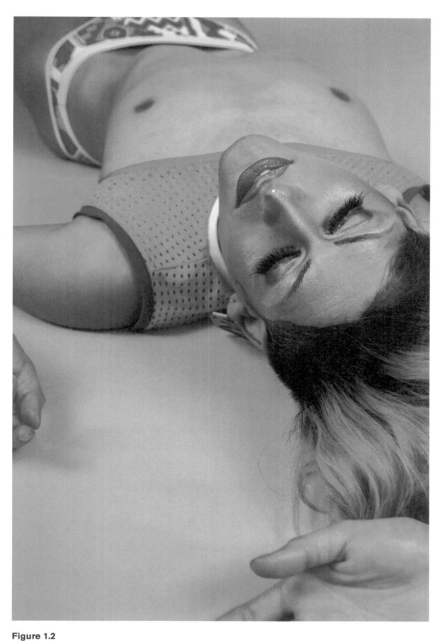

Figure 1.2

Credit: *Rebirth Garments* / Model: Abhijeet Rane / Photo: *Colectivo Multipolar*

The thing that I make the most are chest binders, which are garments used to flatten the chest. I also make a lot of tucking underwear or gaffs, which are bottoms underwear that is made to compress outie bits, like outie genitals. But there are also things like packing underwear, which typically has a pocket or something built in to create a bulge in your pants. There are also bras that have a lot of padding in them or have room for some sort of prosthetic to create more of a chest. These are typically the gender-affirming underwear styles.

But most clothing lines who make this type of stuff are very strict. Even though they cater towards trans folks, they are still stuck in more binary thinking. "This is for trans men," or, "This is for trans women," and they won't really make allowances for nonbinary folks or folks who are just gender-nonconforming or folks who just like the feel of having their chest compressed or things like that.

Most clothing lines tend to use terms like "F to M" or "M to F," which is female-to-male, male-to-female, but I don't like that terminology in the first place. It is weird. It is also saying, they were that kind of person and now they are this particular person. But it is like, they were always this type of person. It is like they are assigned by a doctor a random gender that didn't match their gender identity. I don't like that terminology because of that. I also don't like how binary thinking it is. I wanted to make a clothing line that was totally different.

I wanted to make a clothing line that wasn't strictly for one type of person, because I actually make chest binders for trans women who are on hormones but who might sometimes just want a flatter chest some days. I think that it is cool to be able to have that kind of flexibility to have whatever look that you want.

For some things I design with a type of person in mind. Sometimes I design with trans women or trans feminine or nonbinary folks in mind, but anybody can wear them.

For bottom types of underwear, I always use terms like "innie bits" and "outie bits," so I will be like, "If you have innie bits, it is probably better to have a cotton liner" just because it is healthier for folks with innie bits. Then, if you have outie bits and you want them compressed, you can have this type of liner. If you don't want them compressed, then you can just not have any lining.

What kinds of conversations are you wanting to start with your designs?

I have been working with the Chicago Public Library on an online program called *Radical Fit*, which is a nod to my manifesto, *Radical Visibility*. It wasn't supposed to be online in the first place, but then COVID-19 happened. It is a queer fashion curriculum targeted toward teens. I think we have ninety-one videos for anybody to use, and it isn't just for teens now that is on YouTube. It is for literally anyone. I am really interested in open-source types of stuff.

I feel like the fashion industry has really tricked people into thinking that it is impossible to make your own clothing, even though a hundred years ago we were all making our own clothing or a relative was making your clothing. It's really not as difficult as the fashion industry wants you to believe, but they just want you to believe it so that you are dependent on them, to always buy their stuff, or once something gets messed up, people are like, "Oh, no, I guess I have just got to throw it away." "Get another one."

"No, don't throw it away."

I want people to know that they don't have to go to college to be able to do this. I want people to not feel like they have to necessarily buy into the (in the US) being-in-debt-forever type circle. And, when they do go, some fashion schools are still very much stuck in Eurocentric beauty standards, not allowing for any other types of bodies to be represented.

Radical Fit is all about trying to empower people, and especially teens, to see that it isn't as difficult as the industry makes it out to be. It is also something that you can do as a profession, or it is just a nice life skill.

Where does your distinctive style come from?

I have always loved really bright colors. I love neons, and things like that. And I have also always loved lots of patterns, especially bold geometric patterns, and black and white patterns. Both my parents are artists, and my mom is an amazing dancer and multimedia artist, which is why I like to show my work in dance.

I have been doing a lot of stuff with my father's paintings as patterns for my clothing. Our house is completely covered in them. These 4-foot-long paintings are just super-colorful and geometric, and pretty much all of them have golden ratio, spirals and things like that in them. I started making a bunch of prints with his paintings.

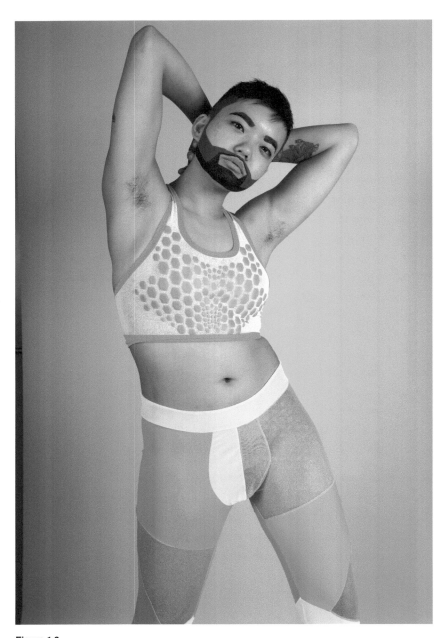

Figure 1.3

Credit: *Rebirth Garments* / Model: Alex Chen / Photo: *Colectivo Multipolar*

I've always been into color. When I was showing my college portfolio, most of them were like: "Ah, too much color" and just freak out. I was like, "Man, this is not even the amount of color that I want."

I just really saw how these places were obsessed with Eurocentric art history and loved minimal colors. It was all minimalism. That was what was considered sleek. That is what was beautiful. I have always been a maximalist and I feel like my parents are both maximalists, too, although I think I am a little more extreme with it. I just really saw how it seemed like classism was tied into also being, "This is what is beautiful." "This is the thing to do." But that is not what I am interested in.

That is not the history of Filipinos or of queer folks. I was, "No, I don't want to be obsessed with this thing that I don't even like at all." Now that I am running my own clothing line, I get to do whatever and just dig in with my own aesthetic.

When people are buying my work, they can order it in any color. I do make a lot of stuff that is all black, but I just like people to be able to have the choice of being colorful or not. So many clothing lines, they don't want you to have the choice, and they are like, "No, this is the only thing that looks good," or, "This is what will look proper" or whatever. I don't care. I will make for people whatever color combo that they want and that they think is cute.

Sometimes I do get quite intense feedback. Sometimes people get so upset about how much color I use. But my whole thing is just letting people have the choice of being able to have whatever colors or styles that they want.

I think about geometry and color being all smashed together. It is very nonbinary. It is very gender nonconforming. I like doing geometric pattern making. I like how it looks. But I think a lot of times people think of geometry as being uncomfortable or something, but I try and make super-comfortable clothing.

I just take zillions of measurements, and then I do all the geometry to make things fit. I have figured out how to pretty much always make things fit really nicely. I also just love thinking about geometry and how it is figuring out how to make things that hug your body comfortably.

Visibility is an important part of many people's creative practice. Why is it important for you and the people you clothe to be radically visible and take up space?

I wanted to imbue my clothing line with the idea of being radically visible, of being totally yourself. Not to assimilate to whatever standards that society is telling us that we have to assimilate to and just taking up visual space and taking up physical space, taking up audio space—just every kind of space, taking it up.

I wanted to imbue my clothing line with the idea of being radically visible, of being totally yourself.

I think the best examples of this are my fashion performances. Instead of a catwalk or a typical fashion show, all of my models are all these marginalized identities. They are all queer or trans or disabled, fat, POC [people of color], intersex, just everything. I make each person their dream outfit from a set of questions, like an interview that I do with each model, and then we dance to show it off. I want to show that people can move in my clothing.

I worked for a very typical fashion brand when I was in high school. They were obsessed with Eurocentric beauty standards, or typical beauty standards, super-skinny, super-tall, super-pale looks. The models couldn't move in the clothing that they made. So, when they had their presentations, they wouldn't even have the models walk. They would just be standing. They couldn't move. This is so ridiculous. Clothing that is expensive that everybody is obsessed with, but you literally can't move in. It is just so awful.

I want people to be comfortable. My stuff is so comfy and soft, and I feel like there is so much unnecessary tightness in a lot of clothing. I am like, "You don't really need this much tightness to keep this clothing on." "Why does it need to be so tight?" I want people to not even notice that they are necessarily wearing clothing, or the clothing is enabling them to do so much more than before. Much of clothing is so restrictive, so I want my clothing to just let people do whatever they need to do and be able to fully move round.

In my shows, each person comes out and they are just dancing and doing whatever they want. I tell them they can literally do anything. They can crawl on the ground, they can roll around, they can be silly or goofy or sexy, or do literally whatever they want. I just want them to dance however they would dance if they were home alone in their bedrooms.

So that is what I do, and I think the shows are really exciting for people, for the models and also for people watching. You get to see all of the queer, and trans, and disabled folks, having pure joy and getting to really move around a stage and take up space and interacting with each other and just being cute. I think it is really fun.

You get to see all of the queer and trans, and disabled folks, having pure joy and getting to really move around a stage and take up space and interacting with each other and just being cute.

How do ideas about representation map on to visibility for you?

I do a lot of stuff with physical visibility or visual visibility. When I started the clothing line, I didn't want it to be just for sighted folks. I think about a lot about other kinds of visibility. At the beginning, I was like, "Ooh, what about texture, taking up space with texture and sound and things like that?" I started a collective called *Radical Visibility Collective*, and that is clothing plus songs that have audio-descriptive lyrics.

I wanted to make sure that there was more representation. I shared my shows with a bunch of people who are more familiar with disability art and audio descriptions and things like that. They were like, "I have never heard audio-descriptive music like this before, this is super-revolutionary," and I was like, "Yes, that is the goal."

Visibility is really important to me. People who are super-revolutionary and life-changing to me were just so amazingly important. I think that if you can have people who are radically visible in any aspect of your life, it can be so life changing. Like getting to see other kinds of people at the grocery store that is by my house. There are a lot of dykes and queers who work there.

Having them in my visual space when I was a teen was really helpful. A lot of them helped me get through my first breakup and things like that. So, I just want to make it more possible for people to be able to see radically visible people or encounter radically visible people in their lives.

I just want to make it more possible for people to be able to see radically visible people or encounter radically visible people in their lives.

Body as Material

Karoline Vitto (she/her/hers)

London, United Kingdom
https://karolinevitto.com

Karoline Vitto is a Brazilian-born womenswear designer whose work represents "the body as material." She accentuates the curves and folds of bodies to celebrate a diversity of shapes from UK sizes 8 to 28. In her design studio in London, Karoline develops size-inclusive womenswear that is shaped by her relationship with her own body, as well as being influenced by other cross-cultural body image concerns. Her designs combine experimental knitwear and elastics with other mixed-media, including delicately formed brass body jewelry. Together these materials play on the concept of restriction and liberation of the flesh by sensuously emphasizing the beauty of the body's rolls and bulges that would traditionally be concealed or compressed.

How did your size-inclusive design practice start and who are you imagining it for?

At first, it was mostly about the relationship I had with my own body. I really wanted to be able to try things on. I wanted to be able to see how they felt and how comfortable they were. I wanted to be able to experience those garments. And obviously, when I say womenswear, I imagine anyone who's got a shape that is curvy, more of a women's traditional kind of figure. It doesn't necessarily mean to be gendered. It's more about biology. We have our deposits of fat in areas that men's bodies don't.

I started to realize that there was space for other genders as well, and that these designs shouldn't be gendered. So, that's something that I want to look at more in the future. It's a bit difficult because when you're working with form, you have those shapes in mind, so it's more about finding the right models who could be male and they could also fit the idea. That's what I'm trying to do.

How does your approach to sizing differ from other clothing designers?

I know many brands want to expand their sizing. But what most do is they have a design that is meant for a [UK] size 8 or for a size 10, and then they simply grade it up. It's like they always start the idea from a smaller body,

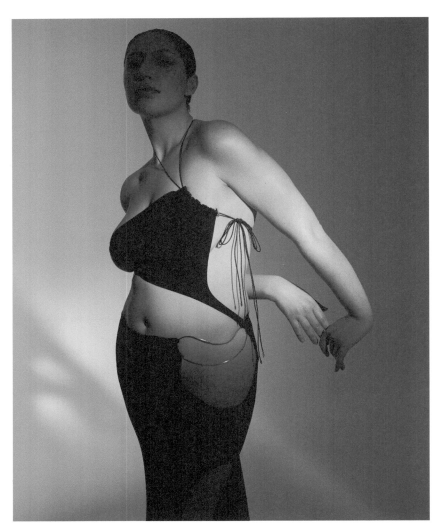

Figure 1.4
Karoline Vitto—SS21 Campaign.
Credit: Karoline Vitto / Photo: Lucas Fonseca / Hair and Makeup Artist: Alex Origuella /
Styling and Model: Karoline Vitto

and then they adapt it. I don't like to do that. So, whenever I have to do something for a larger body, or the way that I sample everything, I sample on an 18 or a 16, and it's mostly because it's been my size for a long time, so I could try them on.

But, I think what's really important is that I don't start at an 8. So, when I'm grading, I only grade a couple of sizes up, a couple of sizes down, and when I sample again, I sample again on a 20, and I sample again on a 26 and so on. The lines change, because suddenly you realize that what you were doing for a certain size doesn't really work in terms of proportion on another size, and that there is something that you can do that is specifically for, let's say a size 24, that would look really beautiful there, but again wouldn't work on a size 8.

I think it's just really important to address that when you're dressing bodies—you have to start from the body. I work with a mannequin but whenever I need to press the body or really emphasize a certain shape, I create layers of wadding so that it's soft, like skin.

For me it's really important to have the idea of gravity, as well. Since I work so much with women who have larger breasts, if you just work with the mannequin, and fiber, and wood, it doesn't have the same effect as breasts have. And if you don't mimic that, you never know how the garment is going to look. I know that, in the summer, they sweat underneath, so it's these things that I feel like, if you haven't experienced this body, it's a little bit more difficult to understand.

So whenever I design for a larger body, I really like to talk to the model, or to the women who I'm designing for, so that I understand these nuances. It's really important to get some answers from them, in terms of what presses and what bothers? "What do you feel here?" "What do you feel there?"

How distinctive is this approach?

There was a commission I had to do for a model who was a size 28, and they wanted something very similar to one of the designs that I already had. And at the time, I was without a studio, and they gave me a short deadline, so I was trying to look for someone who could pattern cut for me, just to speed it up. I tried lots of people that I knew. I tried professionals that I had worked with, and all the sampling studios in London, and everyone would say that they wouldn't do it, because it was very specialized.

They said, "Well, you would have to start everything from scratch, and it would be necessary to do several attempts until we get it right. It's very difficult." The whole purpose of pattern cutting is creating 2D shapes for 3D bodies, and if the 3D body that you can dress only goes up to a certain size, there's this big gap of geometrical knowledge. It's missing.

And when you start to work in that aspect, you start to learn lots of things they really don't teach you when they teach you pattern cutting, because they're not considering plus size bodies. And I'm going to use the word "plus size," even though I don't really agree with it, but just as a general term for understanding it's a larger body. So yes, there's this big, big gap of knowledge, in terms of technical knowledge and also in terms of shape and pattern cutting.

How important is language for describing these missing bodies?
It's been really difficult to find the right words. I try to listen to the women talking about it, because I don't want to say anything that's not going to make sense, or that is going to be hurtful for someone. I think the idea of plus size implies that there's a standard size, so that's what I don't like about it. And you can describe it in more of a plain way, which could be "larger bodies" and "smaller bodies." I tend to use that, but for me it also sounds like there's a standard. I see lots of women prefer the term "curve" or "curvy," so that's the one that I use the most, because it's really descriptive. It's a curvy body.

I really wanted to make women feel better about themselves and be a bit more in control of who they are and what they have to say and what they want to do.

In terms of my practice, this works, because I'm really talking about the curves. However, I have a tiny problem with that as well, because I feel like curvy is associated with something sensual. I tend to prefer that term, but I still find it really difficult. And when I'm trying to talk about my work in Portuguese, it becomes even more difficult. There is this whole group of women who are talking about the use of the words, and then half the women really prefer to be called fat. They say it's a word that's describing their body; it shouldn't be an offence. Some really want to repurpose the word. And in Portuguese, there's not even a word to use when you're describing the rolls on the body. Every word feels really dated, so it's difficult to find a right one.

I think one of the goals that I had, when I started my work, was to really make a difference. I know that sounds very aspirational. Maybe it sounds a little bit dreamy, but I really wanted to make women feel better about themselves and be a bit more in control of who they are and what they have to say and what they want to do.

For me, obviously I want to sell and make money, and I want to be able to live off my brand, like artists and designers. But in a more idealistic kind of way, I think it's really about changing how people perceive their bodies, for the best.

People send me messages: "Oh I felt really conscious about my back rolls, and I saw your pictures." And there was a woman who said, "There was this bodysuit that I had, and I could never wear it because it would show the rolls on my back, so I felt really bad about it, but after I saw your images, and how you thought that was beautiful, I started to look at myself in that way as well." So, for me that's really important. I'm a firm believer that the more you see something, the more you're going to get used to it, and the more you're going to find it beautiful.

I'm a firm believer that the more you see something, the more you're going to get used to it, and the more you're going to find it beautiful.

But, if you're my generation, you grew up with '90s supermodels and their body type, and that type of face, and that type of hair. And even curly hair was a big no in Brazil for many, many years. When I started to see that in the media a lot more, and on the internet, then I was like, "Okay, I actually can accept my hair, I can actually like it." It's this process of resignifying something that wasn't associated with beauty. I think for me it's about that transformation.

Do you see this as a radical act? Why?

I think in the beginning when I started, whenever we had buyers coming into college to give talks and things like that, they would look at our portfolios and comment. And most of the times they would be like, "Oh well, this is really fresh, but you have to make something commercial out of it." They couldn't imagine women wanting to wear something that is going to emphasize their stomach. So, I think in the beginning I still had that view, and I thought, well, you know, this is going to be difficult to sell. This is going to be an idea that is going to work as an image but is not going to work as a product.

And now, I'm really beyond that. I don't really know how to explain how it happened, but I don't see it as unnatural anymore. Maybe that's not the word. Now I find it more normal. I don't know if it's because I saw other people doing something similar, but I feel like people are more accepting of the idea. And I've been approached by a few stores, who think the product is commercial, so maybe that helped. I don't know if I see it as radical anymore, which is a good thing. Because I feel like it should be normal.

I just think we're used to clothes that create an ideal sort of feminine shape—like slim, narrow waist, and everything sort of tucked in. I think for me, it was never really about size, but it was about form. It's almost like you have to be a glass shape. You have to be smooth. So, I think it's about that, and what my clothes do is not repurpose but rather reshape that. I'm cutting the lines around the body, in a way that these areas visually pop out or physically pop out.

Do your designs free bodies and free wearers? Is this how you view them?

Yes, that was the point. When I started, I was looking at elastics and compression elements, and I was trying to explore what they did. They press. They really contain, but they only contain the body to emphasize what's coming out. I think we've been so used to containing and taming. And if we're talking about hair again, I don't know how it was in English-speaking countries, but in Brazil, people used to say, "You need to tame this hair." "It's so offensive." I don't want to tame it. I think it's about the idea that something needs to be under control. Why?

Whenever I go to Brazil, I start to feel really self-conscious about how I look, because everyone there cares so much about workouts, and looking tanned. It's such an intense pressured culture for beauty. I bought a waist cincher. It was made to measure, then I came to London. I tried to put it on and my body was popping out of it. So, that was the starting point. "Okay actually, these shapes are really interesting, and they remind me of what I was doing before." But there is something structural about this, like I was wearing this kind of jersey bra, and a sort of corset type of trainer, and my fat was popping out, so I was like, "There's something that's visually really interesting here." So, that's how I started; I was just curious about the form, and then it evolved.

I think I'm simply acknowledging form that is already there, and shape that is already there, it just wasn't catered for. That's how I see it. I think what's new about it is that I'm acknowledging something that wasn't considered worthy.

If I'm honest, I think there's nothing new about the garments I'm making. Like if I were to dress a size 8 model in all the garments that I make, you would have seen them before—strappy, catsuit, and cutouts. It's not about the clothes, it's about the person that wears them, and the fact that people wouldn't have thought that the people that I dress, would have dressed in the dresses that I'm making. I think that's what's new or fresh about it.

Who is wearing your designs?

The women who buy my clothes or who want to wear them are women who are at a stage where they don't feel bad about themselves. It's not aspirational, in the sense of, "One day I want to look like that." It's like, "Oh, I look like this, I might as well just wear it." It's that kind of feeling. They're not buying for something that they want to belong in. They're not buying into an idea that they're not part of. They are already who they are, and they want something that makes sense to them. I think they just want to feel free to show their bodies, and not to hide them. From what I get from their conversations, they want to show their bodies, and to be able to show it in something that was designed for that body.

I think they just want to feel free to show their bodies, and not to hide them.

I'm not trying to create an aspirational image. I'm trying to reflect what is there. I think that's why it's unapologetic. They're not trying to change. It's not women who are trying to lose weight or who are trying to look different. I'm not trying to hide anything. I'm not trying to disguise anything.

I feel like, whenever women have a chance to feel free, like whenever women have a chance to feel liberated and to feel like they are in control, that is a political act, because society has tried to control women's bodies for so long. And when you control bodies, you control minds, and you control attitudes. And even though it seems like a small act, it isn't, in the larger scope of things.

Dress Tents

Robin Lasser (she/her/hers) and Adrienne Pao (she/her/hers)

California, United States

https://www.dresstents.com

Designed by Robin Lasser and Adrienne Pao, *Dress Tents* are wearable architecture installations of dramatically oversized dresses. For over two decades, they have been staged and photographed worldwide in a range of public spaces such as parks, urban centers, and international borders. Some are designed to be viewed from the outside, while others invite viewers into them. All are created to suit specific contexts of culture and place and to address pressing social issues such as immigration, climate change, colonialism, and women's rights. At times this includes drawing on Robin's Russian and Polish ancestry and Adrienne's Hawaiian heritage. Robin and Adrienne talk with us about the importance of humor, playfulness, the scale of their designs, and the impact *Dress Tents* have on participants.

What are *Dress Tents* and what was the idea behind them?

Adrienne: What if women could be completely self-sufficient? What if they could carry their homes on their backs anywhere they went? What if they could take everything they need with them, pitch a tent, and be self-sufficient anywhere they wanted to go? *Dress Tents* are based on this playful idea and on contemporary feminist ideology.

We wanted to bring that visual to life in a photograph. So, we started thinking, let's work with a theater costume sewer and get some garments together that have a significance to us and see if we can make something from this idea of wearable architecture. Let's try three of these together. That was the beginning of it. And here we are, over eighteen years later.

Why did you start with a dress?

Adrienne: We wanted to start with something that was iconographically associated with the dress. And something that we could play with that had a lot of significance throughout time to women. Those garments really represent different social issues, status, requirements, etc.

Robin: Some of our dresses are 20 feet high, and they cascade down into an architectural form. For us, that form is sometimes based on fashion, like the *Missionary MuuMuu Dress Tent*, and relate to how the missionaries in

Hawaii implemented the MuuMuu as a way to cover up native women. But sometimes the forms are based on local architectural elements. In Russia, the shape of the *Dress Tent* was based on the onion-shaped domes seen on top of cathedrals. So, we model the *Dress Tents* on iconic architecture and fashion in the places they are installed. And sometimes we work with the land itself. The *Lava Tube Top Dress Tent*, for example, is made in a way to tip our hat to the geologic formations of the lava flows in Hawaii.

Adrienne: That one was a reference to geography and we were thinking of the ideology and importance of Pele [Goddess of volcanoes and fire], in Hawaiian culture. Also, we found fabric that looked like flowing lava.

Robin: All of the *Dress Tents* are a conflation of fashion, architecture, performance art, photography, and place. In some of the projects, we're looking at social justice issues; other *Dress Tents* grapple with environmental justice and public health issues. There's a sense of play and wonder, magic that we hope to imbue in these installations. It's a kind of upbeat way of looking at topics that sometimes we choose to turn away from. For some of the harder topics, sometimes using a sense of humor or a sense of wonder, can provide a bridge for our audience.

All of the Dress Tents are a conflation of fashion, architecture, performance art, photography, and place. In some of the projects, we're looking at social justice issues; other Dress Tents grapple with environmental justice and public health issues.

What role does scale play in the project?

Robin: I think every single piece we've done has an element of claiming public space for public expression. And when you're working outside, scale is important. I suppose you could do something very miniature, dense, and powerful, because it's so small and intimate. Or do the reverse because you're in competition with the redwood trees and large architectural elements. And by competition, I mean, you're in concert with them.

We're always thinking about those relationships. And photographically, we're aware of how the proximity of the lens always informs scale. When I teach photography, sometimes when I'm chatting with my students, I say if

Figure 1.5
Edible Garden Dress Tent, installed at Montalvo Arts Center, Saratoga, California. 36"W × 30"H, chromogenic print, 2011.
Credit: Robin Lasser + Adrienne Pao / Commissioned by: Montalvo Arts Center / www.DressTents.com

you get low and below something and you shoot up at a person, it's a way for them to visually claim power and respect. So, for me, scale is critical. Making things larger than life is critical when working in a vast landscape.
Adrienne: Typically, we work with tent forms or covers that are made for camping. Some we've designed from scratch, but 80 percent are forms that are typical camping forms, tunnels, and tents that you would use outside. So, we're working from a scale that is larger than life already, as they're meant to cover multiple people.

Why are playfulness, humor, and wonder so important in your work?
Adrienne: When we started this, we knew that we were going to be exploring some topical issues that could have a challenging nature. And we wanted to

do something that could invite people, in a positive way, to explore issues that may be challenging to them. I think that having a sense of humor in art is so needed and exciting. And when there's a playfulness to art, people can take a delight in it. Art is fun. And we wanted to have fun doing these. And we just wanted to bring that lightness to it.

We wanted to do something that could invite people in a positive way, to explore issues that may be challenging to them. I think that having a sense of humor in art is so needed and exciting.

Adrienne: In terms of the wonder, it was really important for people, from like two years old to one hundred, to have an experience and be able to look at these and be like, "Oh, my goodness, I know what they're talking about." Or, just to have a moment that takes you out of your everyday existence—to have a moment of wonder. I think that having a relationship to humor and creating them as a spectacle, as a form that would stop somebody and create a moment of delight, is something that was important to me as an artist.

Robin: We treat the exterior of these pieces as wearable architecture. So, in your everyday life, if you're in Brazil, and you're going to the marketplace, and you run across one of our *Dress Tents*, you stumble upon it. It is a spectacle drawing your attention. For me, that's the most interesting way for these pieces to work. Then, the interior environment is meant to provide more of a sense of place to contemplate, for deep listening, for meditation.

How has the *Dress Tents* project developed over time?

Adrienne: We've been working on the project for many years and it's taken different iterations over time, of course. When we started, they were primarily based on stereotypical garments that have had a dominant presence in women's lives at some point. And then over the years, they've transitioned from being garments that would be recognizable from womenswear into other things that have cultural significance.

Robin: Earlier ones also took on the geopolitics of place. *Ms. Homeland Security: Illegal Entry Dress Tent* was created in 2005 at the border of Mexico and the US and provided an opportunity to think about border issues, whether they're geographically or psychologically located.

Figure 1.6

Sari Dress Tent, installed in front of the San Francisco City Hall. 48"W × 40"H, chromogenic print, 2019.

Credit: Robin Lasser + Adrienne Pao / Commissioned by the Asian Art Museum in San Francisco, California / www.DressTents.com

Adrienne: *Dress Tents* have taken different inspiration sources, based on what we're working on at that time. We photographed them at the beginning, primarily in California and Hawaii. And the reason Hawaii came into it was because my dad's side of the family is from Hawaii, we wanted to explore that place. And as the project has grown, we've done them in lots of different places, always working with the people in the place to collaborate and bring something to life that is relevant to that community.

Robin: We did a piece in Russia titled *Ms. Yekaterinburg: Camera Obscura Dress Tent*. Like Adrienne with Hawaii, for me, my ancestry is Russian and Polish. So, it's a way to reenter our personal histories and have time to work with and examine our contemporary relationships to those cultures.

Dress Tents get exhibited as large-scale photographs because we feel that what we're creating is a conflation between that installation and the geopolitics of the space in which it's located. So, the photograph is a way of marrying the two.

How do you work with different communities?

Robin: *Dress Tents* also provide venues for other people's stories. In the *Dress Tent* commissioned by Governor Newsom in California, we were charged with representing the city of San José. Why San José? We both have affiliations to this city. I have been a professor of art at San José State University for the last thirty years. Adrienne is an alum of there as well. And so, we both have important ties to that city. And it's home to a large population of Vietnamese Americans and Latinx communities. We were charged to work around COVID-19 and Adrienne came up with this idea. "We all have been living in our bubbles." So, we decided to create two tents, one for each community, based loosely on or inspired by the bubble as the architectural element and traditional clothing from Vietnam and Mexico as the fashion.

Then we created messages that have to do with our emergence from the pandemic like, "Vaccinated, no more loneliness," or "Wearing a mask expresses love," in these two different languages. And for the Latinx community, we chose papel picado as the vehicle for messaging. Papel picado are paper banners with cutouts. They don't always have textual messages, but they're like banners, and they feel celebratory. We wanted this emergence from the pandemic to feel celebratory.

Dress Tents were worn and performed by members of the community in public spaces in San José. These community-engaged photoshoot events evolved into a set of twelve unique billboards installed throughout the city. Thus, the work goes out into the public once again. So even if they get shown in museums and other places at a later time, I think we're always cognizant of our desire to make the work available to the general public, utilizing public space for public expression.

We're always cognizant of our desire to make the work available to the general public, utilizing public space for public expression.

Figure 1.7
Ms Homeland Security: Illegal Entry Dress Tent, installed beneath the California/Mexico border fence. 48"W × 40"H, chromogenic print, 2005.
Credit: Robin Lasser + Adrienne Pao / www.DressTents.com

What kinds of feedback do you get from people who experience your work?
Robin: Some of the *Dress Tents* are more performative than others. The *Sari Dress Tent*, with her 30-foot elongated pallu [loose end of a sari worn over the shoulder], was installed and photographed in front of the San Francisco City Hall. It is often where people end up at the end of protest marches and that kind of thing. At the time, we were thinking about immigration and immigrants to our country.

On three different occasions I created projects for global festivals in India. The *Sari Dress Tent* was performed by Kathak dancers. Kathak are traditional nature dances from India. The dancers were young people from high school, trained beautifully by a choreographer. And thirty women donated their saris. They said, "Every sari has a story."

We draped the saris inside the *Dress Tent*, and with the light pouring in, it felt like being in a chapel with stained glass windows. And these thirty women shared their stories: "This sari I wore at the birth of my son," or "At my father's funeral," and that kind of thing. You heard this collection of stories inside the tent, and you could try to imagine which sari was associated with which story. As photographers, ways of seeing have always been an integral part of our creative process.

You talked earlier of your desire to serve the public. Why is it so important?
Robin: I think it goes back to the recognition that all we have in life is each other. We are seeking love and giving love. I feel one of the ways we do this is by providing story-sharing venues. I feel that the more we have compassion for each other and everything living on this planet, the more we'll be aware of, and champion, a sustainable way of living.

Adrienne: I think it's important to amplify voices in our society. As Robin said, some of these are our stories. Some of these are others' stories. We are fortunate to be able to work with those communities and be able to aid in amplifying those stories as well. As we've grown in the work and have specific engagements with particular communities, it has become more and more important and valuable to have relationships with people and to provide work that serves an audience that is well beyond mine or Robin's.

Also, it's all really inspirational. An exciting part of the project is to get to work with so many different communities and people. It is very important to us to provide space for everybody as best we can. Because it's a gift. I think it's a gift to be able to give something, and to be able to get to work with communities like we're doing right now.

Third Thumb, Vine Arm, Materialise Arm, and Synchronised Arm

Dani Clode (she/her/hers)

London and Cambridge, United Kingdom
https://www.daniclodedesign.com/

Working as *Dani Clode Design*, Dani Clode is an augmentation designer and researcher exploring the future of the body. Originally from New Zealand, she completed an MA in Design Products at the Royal College of Art (RCA) and works on multidisciplinary collaborative projects in London and Cambridge. Dani collaborates with neuroscientists to explore the brain's ability to adapt to controlling different prosthetic body parts. She researches, designs, publishes and exhibits her work around the world. Here, she shares insights into the potential of the expanding human body in multiple projects: *Third Thumb*, *Vine Arm*, *Materialise Arm*, and *Synchronised Arm*.

How is the body central to your practice?

I aim to challenge the perception and boundaries of prosthetic design and extend the human form. I incorporate new materials and design processes, inspired by the mechanics of the human body and robotics. I've designed objects that mediated interaction, but I was unsatisfied with buttons and switches; I wanted to work instead with the surface of the body. I found that prosthetics were a perfect crossover to all my interests into developing a unique relationship and interface with a product, whilst engaging with new materials.

Prosthetics are about this constant iteration with new technologies: constantly trying to make things better, and still kind of falling short of how amazing the human body is. It's so challenging and compelling to be aiming for a goal that's constantly moving and growing. When it comes to working with the body, just the sheer number of different shapes and sizes and everything that the body comes in just fascinates me. But we're also at a point now where we can start to think beyond the body as well, that we're not restricted by trying to re-create how the body is currently designed.

We're also at a point now where we can start to think beyond the body as well, that we're not restricted by trying to re-create how the body is currently designed.

What is the difference between augmentation and prosthetics?

I personally don't see a difference between augmentation and prosthetics. I know that's not a popular opinion but it's something that is very crucial to my design approach. This is a question I get constantly get asked with my *Third Thumb* design. Is it a prosthetic? Does it replace a missing thumb? Or is it augmentation? Does it extend? And my answer is, "It's both." It's always been both. It just depends on where you put it, who you put it on, and your perspective of what a "regular" body is. I've worked with so many different shaped hands, numbers of fingers, and arms, and when you attach a piece of technology that extends the wearer's ability, that's awesome, but what you call that technology depends on your perspective of the person or how they view or define themselves.

In collaboration with Sophie de Oliveira Barata and *The Alternative Limb Project*, I've designed three arms for model and activist Kelly Knox—who was born with one arm—and for her, these arms were extra and conceptual. I've never seen Kelly as missing anything, she is her full self, that's how she was born. So, the three prosthetic arm designs Sophie and I made for her were so fun and trippy. We got to push the boundaries of what a prosthetic is or can be, because the function was to just be a physical, interactive extension of Kelly.

And joining The Plasticity Lab, originally at the Institute of Cognitive Neuroscience at University College London, and now at the MRC Cognition and Brain Sciences Unit at Cambridge University, I am working with the amazing Prof. Tamar Makin. I'm seeing this other side of prosthetics and augmentation research and finding and discussing neuroscience research that scientifically supports what I've felt, being an emotive designer working with people and the body.

And what I'm learning is that the brain doesn't really know that there's meant to be two arms. The regions in the brain linked to arm movement develop through use. And with congenital one-handers, they won't have a specifically "left hand" region of the brain if they didn't physically develop an arm, because their brain uses that space for other functions. With amputees, it's different because they've gone through a trauma, and can experience a phantom limb and sometimes phantom pain. But again, these are two different types of people, with completely different experiences. With the

Figure 1.8
The *Third Thumb* project.
Credit: *Dani Clode Design* / daniclode.com

Figure 1.9
The *Third Thumb* project.
Credit: *Dani Clode Design* / daniclode.com

Third Thumb collaboration with the Plasticity Lab, we are focusing more on augmentation defined as an addition to the body. We're exploring how the brain responds to a completely new body part.

Can you tell us more about some of these designs?

The *Third Thumb* is a 3D printed thumb extension for your hand, controlled by your big toes. With the Thumb, it was really about understanding the relationship that forms between the wearer and their prosthetic, and also trying to reframe how we speak about prosthetics.

The *Third Thumb* is currently part of exciting new neuroscientific research. We're looking into the relationship between augmentation and the brain, and so now I get to make *Third Thumbs* for my day job, which is awesome. From a neuroscientific perspective, human augmentation is interesting because it is a great model for studying the boundaries of brain plasticity. What we wanted to find out is whether it is even possible to merge augmentative technology with the human body. Because these technologies are advancing so rapidly, what we still don't know is whether our brains can actually support them. Can the human brain properly support an extra body part? And how can using that extra body part impact the control of our biological body?

In our first study, published in *Science Robotics*, we trained people to use the *Third Thumb* over five days and looked at how learning to use this new body part affects neural body representation.[17] The thing that is really unique about our study is that this is the first time we have actually been able to allow people to use an augmentative device outside of the lab and see how taking advantage of the extra thumb changes the way people use their hands, which we see change in the brain. We found that people can quickly learn to control an augmentation device, and use it for their benefit, without overthinking. But we also found that using an extra thumb is not neutral to the brain; there is a trade-off. In order for people to use the augmentative technology efficiently, they need to change the way they use their natural fingers; they need to create new movement synergies, and by doing that, they update the way their body is represented in the brain. And we found that this is a very important message for everyone interested in safe and successful motor augmentation—it may incur changes to how the brain represents our bodies—and we need to better understand these potential changes for the future of augmentative design.

How important is it for you to work closely with the people who use your designs?

Working with Kelly Knox, who is a model and body confidence advocate, and making arms for her, really helped Sophie and I reimagine and reframe what prosthetics are when the focus isn't a moving human-shaped hand. Because Kelly chooses to not wear a prosthetic in her daily life, the design brief became something different, which was fascinating.

The *Synchronised Arm* was about flipping the focus—to show Kelly's actual arm shape within the socket. The usual focus of a prosthetic arm is the hand because it's usually a robotic hand or a hook, and the socket is secondary, and completely covers the arm. We decided to completely flip this focus. What if the hand was the least important thing, and the most important thing was the actual end of Kelly's arm? We made the socket purely shaped around her own arm, and then electroplated it in gold. We 3D scanned her right arm and mirrored it and re-created it 1:1 in clear layered acrylic. I also designed a layer of the acrylic to "tick" in time to her heartbeat to try out a new kind of connection for Kelly and the piece; it also continues to tick when Kelly is not wearing it, which creates a lasting connection when there is no longer a physical one. Then everything else became secondary—the hand was even removable. For Kelly, it was an extension of her but not overpowering, and it was beautiful. She had a challenging relationship with prosthetics growing up. So this piece was about celebrating *her* arm.

Our second piece we worked on with Kelly was the *Materialise Arm*, and this was to really push the boundaries and challenge the current aesthetics and materiality of prosthetics.

It's divided into two main sections, part skin-like silicone, part mixed materials—which are also interchangeable. The arm is made from over twenty different materials ranging from hand-finished wood, pumice, and cork—to 3D printed resins, plastics, and plated bronze. And not only do the interchangeable elements allow for different aesthetics for Kelly to choose from

Figure 1.10
Synchronised Arm.
Credit: *The Alternative Limb Project*, *Dani Clode Design* & Jason Taylor / Photo: Omkaar
Kotedia / Model: Kelly Knox / thealternativelimbproject.com

depending on how she feels, but they also change the texture and weight of
the arm.

The skin side of *Materialise* was expertly crafted by my collaborator
Sophie, and it was to help to form a strong visual connection and recognition
between Kelly and the object.

This was actually Kelly's favorite arm by far, and she said, "I felt like it
was part of me, not separate . . . which was totally unexpected!!" And this
was awesome—coming from someone who chooses not to wear a prosthetic
in daily life.

The *Vine Arm* was inspired by a mood board Kelly made. She's an awesome trippy person and it was all kind of extra-terrestrial and we were just
trying to piece together something really cool. Some of the other mood
boards she'd made for us were nature based as well, so we decided to merge
them. The *Vine* is made up of twenty-six individual vertebrae that are controlled by four pressure sensors imbedded in Kelly's shoes, situated above

Figure 1.11
The *Materialise Arm*.
Credit: *The Alternative Limb Project*, *Dani Clode Design* & Jason Taylor / Photo: Simon Clemenger / Model: Kelly Knox / thealternativelimbproject.com

Figure 1.12
The *Vine Arm*.
Credit: *The Alternative Limb Project*, *Dani Clode Design*, Jason Taylor & Hugo Elias / Photo: Omkaar Kotedia / Model: Kelly Knox / thealternativelimbproject.com

and below her big toes. With this piece we also tied it back to Kelly, through constructing the external shape of the *Vine* and vertebrae by extending the end of Kelly's biological arm, so the underlying *Vine* structure is from her body—as if she grew it. The control was very much connected as well, in that she had proportional control over the *Vine*, through the sensors in her shoes. But what I found fascinating, especially since starting the *Third Thumb* research, is that with this design, we were changing the types of interactions she could have with her environment, and ultimately completely altering the way she was moving her biological body to collaborate with an extension of her.

What kind of a future are you envisioning through your work?
One of my best mates (Lisa Mandemaker) is a speculative designer and we talk a lot about the future of different technologies, and her favorite answer to a lot of questions is, "Which future? There are a lot." I think we are absolutely at the beginning of the journey of adding interactive, embodied technology to the body, and more importantly at the absolute beginning of researching and understanding the effects it will have on our bodies and more importantly our brains. I really enjoy creating research tools to help us to better understand our future selves as well as design catalysts and interactions that generate thought and conversation about the future beyond our bodies.

2 MOVING

1n 1912, Baron Pierre de Coubértin, founder of the International Olympics Committee, argued that women's athleticism "should be excluded from the Olympic program" as he believed it would be "impractical, uninteresting, ungainly," and "improper."[1] He was aware that women enjoyed playing sports, but he did not think audiences would want to watch them. Rather, he believed the Olympic Games were created for "the solemn and periodic exaltation of male athleticism" with "the applause of women as reward." Reflecting on this, sporting historian Jennifer Hargreaves writes, "From the start, the modern Olympics was a context for institutionalised sexism, severely hindering women's participation," and much work has been needed to challenge this "powerful conservatising force."[2] This long-term marginalization and exclusion of women and girls has had wide-ranging impact on their freedom to participate not only in sport but also more generally in their ability to lead active public lives.

Sport is often seen as a symbol of citizenship and national identity. Worldwide events like the Olympics have long celebrated heroism, strength, daring, risk, and triumph. Central to these spectacles are idealized, cisgendered, unimpaired bodies. For centuries, athletes of different sizes, abilities, and ethnicities have struggled against these conventions and narratives. To be involved, "they have had to challenge, resist or work around prevailing ideas that many sports and physical activities are inappropriate and incompatible with their bodies."[3] Feminist historian Natasha Vertinsky reminds us that the andronormative bias is based on a long-held "pervasive notion that should a woman step beyond the formula of correct, moderate and systematic exercise she might encounter physical, mental and moral dangers."[4] Although much has changed over the past century, sporting inequalities still play out in everyday contexts as well as in international competition.

These attitudes continue to shape and limit who feels safe, comfortable, and welcome to move in and through public space. Reports by sporting organizations and charities evidence a myriad of reasons for these inequities. A 2022 study by *Sport England*, for example, found far more girls than boys in Britain stop feeling "sporty" as they grow into adulthood.[5] Their diminished interest in sports at school reduced their physical activity later in life. One of the report's key recommendations is to expand the image of "what 'sporty' looks like."[6] Wearables are a key site of contention within the context of sport because having inappropriate or ill-fitting equipment can limit or prevent participation. As in other areas of life, a lack of diverse representation can be alienating to those who do not see themselves reflected in the provisions on offer. Body shapes, hair styles, and religious and cultural requirements (such as modest attire) that differ from narrowly-defined defaults are rarely given equal attention by the media or sports brands.

Additionally, some people are disproportionately targeted with criticism, ostracism, and physical and administrative violence when they engage in sport and other physical activity. For example, at the time of writing, manufactured and unsubstantiated moral panics concerning transgender athletes were being amplified by the media and politicians, resulting in bans from amateur as well as professional sporting events.[7]

This chapter focuses on innovative wearables for all kinds of moving bodies. Throughout this book, all bodies are bodies in motion, but here we explore inventive wearables for sporting and active people worn in public. We're interested in how designers identify, work around, or directly challenge restrictive social conventions about who is enabled, encouraged, or permitted to be active. The following designs focus on a wide range of sporting and active bodies: modest activewear that particularly benefits Muslim girls and women to antiharassment cyclewear and DIY patterns for everyday activewear. All the designers translate political ideas of representation into material forms, offering ways for a wider range of people to more fully participate in public active life.

We start with the origin story of the *Burqini*: modest all-over body-covering swimwear designed by **Aheda Zanetti**, of *Ahiida*. Aheda explains how her niece struggled to play netball in scorching summer heat while wearing a conventional hijab. Unable to find anything suitable for her to wear, she combined her skills, commitment, and cultural influences to design a modest sports garment. This swiftly turned into the *Burqini*, addressing the gap for modest swimwear. It became part of the uniform adopted by the Australian Surf Life Saving Association, a uniquely Australian institution, and is loved by people from different backgrounds all around the world. Aheda is still amazed by its global impact: "It was a lot of hard work . . . from the moment I started, all I ever did was fight—fight for the defense of rights." For over twenty years, she has transformed girls' and women's sport and positively shaped attitudes toward Muslim culture.

We move from the world stage to everyday active lives with **Melissa Fehr**, founder of *Fehr Trade*, who designs digital sewing patterns for activewear. To her, all bodies are potentially active bodies. She explains, "We've got to get rid of those old notions of what it means to be active and what it means to be exercising." Melissa is a firm believer in the idea that "if you have a body, you can exercise." Through providing a range of digital sewing patterns for all kinds of activewear and bodies, Melissa teaches people how to customize items as needed for their body shapes. As she says, "I am more interested in what my body can do, not what my body looks like." Melissa has created an option that not only enables people to create bespoke wearables but also counters the shame of bodies not fitting the athletic ideals represented by mainstream commercially available garments.

Ester van Kempen takes the idea of equal representation out onto the street on her bicycle with the inclusive brand *Ride With Wolves*. Frustrated with the lack of women's cycling clothing and the way the cycling industry in London was dominated by men, she started to make her own cycling clothing with a group of friends. Together, they made a cyclewear collection for all genders and body types. They took inspiration from conversations with other underrepresented cyclists about how they sometimes felt harassed on the streets. In response, they printed bold antiharassment slogans in retro-reflective ink, which shone brightly under street and car headlights.

Ester explains, "It was a way of taking back that strength, because when you get harassed you kind of lose a bit of yourself, you suddenly feel very small and you're scared, and by doing this clothing line, it really felt like we were taking back the power and our own energies." Reflecting responses back to perpetrators alleviated some of the trauma of urban harassment.

Exploring how to reclaim public space is central to the work of **Nicolas Moser** and his team of architects and designers at *Multiply Office*. One of their many interests lies in provocative uses of public space, made more topical by COVID-19 social distancing measures that limited how citizens could move and get close to each other. Nicolas explains, "We approach every project as an opportunity to better understand what is happening around us and how we can be part of it." He shares two projects that seek to expand personal and private ways for citizens to participate in public life. *Urban Blanket* maps out a place for people to dwell in public. *Petticoat Dress*, in the form of a wide colorful skirt, aimed to rework COVID-19 social distancing guidelines into more poetic, choreographed, and playful ways of interacting with each other and being in the city.

Collectively, this chapter showcases imaginative ways designers have identified and attempted to reconfigure limiting issues and negative narratives with new practices and expanded expressions of active citizenship. Freedom to be "sporty" and active might seem to relate to only a small part of public life. Yet it matters in, and outside, specific sporting contexts for people's health and safety, sense of autonomy and independence, and civic participation. The following creative responses not only shape the lives of individual wearers but also work to expand possibilities of social and cultural interactions in public space.

Burqini

Aheda Zanetti (she/her/hers)

Sydney, Australia
https://ahiida.com

Lebanese-born Australian designer Aheda Zanetti is the founder of *Ahiida* and inventor of the *Burqini/Burkini* (she owns the patent). *Burqinis* are modest all-over body-covering swimwear, originally designed in response to the lack of appropriate sportswear for Muslim girls and women. As a result of vast media interest and growing awareness of ultraviolet (UV) sun damage, *Burqinis* are now worn by all kinds of active people—Muslim and non-Muslim—around the world. Here, Aheda shares not only the inspiring story behind the initial impetus to design the *Burqini* and its enduring popularity, but also talks with us about the role wearables play in positively expanding people's lives.

The *Burqini* has achieved remarkable global success. Can you tell us how it all started?

I design it. I produce it. I market it. I wear it. I endorse it. I love it. I sew it. I produce it. I mean I eat and drink *Burqini* swimwear. But I'm a mother of four. That's my life. My youngest was three months old when I initially started on the design.

It all started when my sister asked me to come and attend a netball game that my niece was playing in. My niece was quite young at the time, and I remember that it was a really hard struggle to get her into netball, because my niece chose to wear hijab at a very young age. She was the youngest in my whole family. She was probably about eight years old when she chose to wear that hijab, and it was her choice. Her mother never wore it. We never wore it.

But she was also very active. It took them a long time to find a team that would allow her to wear pants, a long-sleeve top, and a hijab underneath their sports team uniform. In fact, the whole Netball Association wouldn't allow it, so there was a bit of a debate in regard to why not, how, what, and whatever. She eventually won the case, but then it was a struggle trying to find a team that would accept her.

Anyway, long story short, they found the team. It was her first game and it was a really, really warm day. We were watching and she's really quite pale, and so, when she was playing, her face was like a tomato. It was so, so red. But she was so happy playing.

Of course, she was the only one that was fully covered, with her team uniform on top. I was thinking, "Oh, my God, this is definitely not suitable." Even her hijab was quite thick. It wasn't comfortable while she was playing.

So, that's what got me thinking. I'd always wanted to play netball as a kid. But I was a bit overweight. Plus, at the same time, those netball uniforms were short. My parents would never have allowed it. Even though we didn't wear hijab, we were always modest.

I went home after my niece's netball match without actually talking to anyone about it. In those days, we had dial-up internet. No one ever wanted to use the computer, because, by the time you'd downloaded something, it would take you all day. But it just got on my mind. So, I waited until everyone went to bed. I wanted to research about it and find out what's going on overseas. "Has anyone ever discovered modest sportswear?" If there is something, maybe I'll look into it and purchase something for my niece.

Of course, there wasn't, and it just got me researching a little bit more. Lots of people were talking about it. But no one was really listening. Anyway, I just looked, and looked, and looked, and looked. God, I looked for weeks. Then one day I thought, "Will I . . . ?"

There are clearly lots of social, political, and cultural influences in your designs. Can you explain more about how they came together?
Even though I was born in Lebanon, and I have my Arab culture within me, I am really also very Australian as well. So, I really wanted to blend in with the culture, with the lifestyle. I didn't want to be Muslim, non-Muslim. . . .

Women and girls that want to participate in sport really don't want to be labeled by anything except their activity. That's one of the biggest reasons why I wanted it to blend in with a Western style of clothing. Also, I hate pins and excess fabrics. I'm not that type of person. I wanted it to be easy; easy to put on, easy to put up. You didn't have to worry about if you had a pin. You didn't have to worry about if you had an elastic band.

I first designed the cap so you wouldn't have to worry. I've got long hair, and I didn't want to worry if I had an elastic band or not. It was going to be secure, no matter what. It had enough room if I decided to grow my hair. I also designed it to be sleek. There was no excess fabric. I could do handstands and it wouldn't move.

I then made a sports garment for my niece. I didn't want anyone to change any sports team, because, once you start asking them for change, they'll start: "It's another Muslim wanting another change." I didn't want to step on anyone's toes, so it had to be just an undergarment. Put it on. Take it off. That's it, easy. It catered for our local soccer teams and netballers. They were also playing cricket, but that's about it. There was not much going on in regard to sports.

How did this turn into the *Burqini*?

It turned into the *Burqini* very quickly because I'm a swimmer. I love swimming. I needed different fabric technology to make sure it wasn't going to be heavy, it wasn't going to drag. It is a full garment.

One of the problems was the veil. If women went into water, their veil was going to slip off, especially underwater. So, everything on this garment has a purpose. The chin part is to make sure that it is always going to stay in place. This part at the back is going to give you the excess for your hair. The band is going to keep your headband secure. Everything on the garment had a reason. That's how it started.

In those days, for Muslims, as long as you were covered, that's all right. That's it. Don't worry about how you feel. Don't worry about if it's hot, or cold, or whatever. It doesn't matter. But no, I didn't want that to happen. I wanted to make sure not only that you were covered, if you choose to be modest or you choose to veil, but that you were also going to be extremely comfortable wearing it.

I wanted to make sure not only that you were covered, if you choose to be modest or you choose to veil, but that you were also going to be extremely comfortable wearing it.

So, I started researching fabrics. "What does 'breathability' mean? What does 'anti-wicking' mean?" I looked around for fabrics. "Where can I buy them? Where are the samples? How do they feel? How much stretch do they need?" That was probably my biggest research in regard to learning and studying about fabrics, because I really wanted it to be comfortable.

What was happening in the world at the time? How did this shape your designs?

I think it would have been about the time September 11 happened. There was a lot of negativity around. I could see a lot of girls that are really not confident. A lot of girls are really smart. They continue school. They go to year 12 [final year of secondary education in Australia]. They probably even go to university, but they're not in the workforce. They end up being back at home, getting married young, and really not having their own identity. They were never part of any sporting activity at school. That's probably what started it off.

And when I was a kid, I was overweight, so I had body issues. There was nothing really that catered for me. Everything I've ever had to do I've had to alter and fix. That's probably what got me started in dressmaking. I'm a self-taught dressmaker and I've been dressmaking since I was ten. It has always been a hobby but a necessity all my life. I'm only 4′9″, so I'm tiny, so it's something I've always had to do. I've always had to find a solution for my body. I think that's probably what brings out who I am now. I'm a fixer. I find solutions for women who are overweight, or underweight, or short and tall. There's always a solution.

I just had my two girls. They were only babies at the time. I thought to myself, "I can't help the world, but what I can do is assist my kids if they chose to wear hijab or whatever they want to do." I never wanted them to miss out on any sporting activity or any school activity. I wanted to do it and I did.

I truly didn't expect that I was going to change the world. What I wanted to do was to make sure that it catered for my niece, and my sisters. Who would have thought it went frigging crazy like that? Who would have thought? Never in my wildest dreams did I ever expect that—never.

Figure 2.1
Burqini–modest swimwear for women and girls.
Credit: Aheda Zanetti / *Ahiida*

What happened?

The first order I received was in the UK. It was mainly all international. They loved it and I thought, "Wow, fantastic." Then Surf Life Saving Australia[8] approached us. I'm sure it was a marketing gimmick of some kind because of the Cronulla riots[9] and so forth, so they wanted to introduce more Muslim boys and girls into the Surf Life Saving program.

"We found out about your Burqini. Would you be able to produce something for us?"

I said, "Yes, no problem," which I did.

It went crazy. I thought, "What the hell?" I couldn't believe how it went viral. The website shut down completely. All the orders were coming through and I couldn't fulfill anything.

I think I nearly went through a nervous breakdown. I couldn't believe it. I couldn't even supply. At the time, I was still making them myself. I was working all night, so my husband used to come home from work, and I would feed the kids and get them all ready for bed. Then I used to go to a little shop that I had and sew all night and come back at 3:00 in the morning. In those days, it was very difficult for me to find anyone to sew the garment.

There are a few techniques in regard to the sewing aspect of it. There's a little pulling and stretching in some parts. Everything has to fit like a glove. Anything that's big or too small, you'll be able to notice it. It has to fit like a puzzle.

What an incredible reaction. Can you share some of the interactions you've had with people?

One of the biggest questions was, "Is this going to stick to my body?" They wanted me to give them the right answer for them to buy it. They really wanted to go and swim, and be active, but they were so unsure, Islamically, if that was the correct thing to do.

But, mind you, Islamically you are required to learn how to swim. It's a life skill. It's actually encouraged in our books. I think it's archery, swimming, and horse riding. So, it's not like we're not allowed to swim. We just never had anything to wear to swim.

Figure 2.2
A Muslim lifesaver wears a Burqini on North Cronulla Beach, Sydney.
Photo by Matt King/Getty Images News via Getty Images

I remember this story. I was in the store once, and there was a lady that came in and said that she wanted to swim. Of course, it was the same story. They've never swum before and they want to enter into the water with their family. They're going on holidays, and this will be the first time that they're actually swimming with their kids—fantastic.

We'd just brought out the plus-size swimwear, so for size 18 and above. She purchased one and she was happy. Everything was fine. She was a bit nervous and she left it at that. Two weeks later, she comes in. She walks in the door and she's crying—like really crying. It's not like tears, it's crying!

The first thing that crossed my mind is, "What have I done?" I thought, "Oh, my God, did something happen on holidays?"

"Take a seat. Come and sit down, Sister. Sit down, sit down."

Anyway, I calmed her down and she goes: "It was the best time of my life." For the first time, she enjoyed her holiday. She participated with her kids and her husband. And her husband and her were all lovey-dovey again.

It was just an amazing reaction. I think that's when I realized, "Wow. What have I done?" I haven't done this. It wasn't me. God just chose me, but I just couldn't believe it. I thought, "Wow, look at the change." That was just one story, but there were thousands of the same.

The good thing about it, is that I think more girls are participating in sporting and swimming, which they've never done before. Private schools—the religious private schools where everything is a no-no—they've now accepted and do swimming lessons for girls, which is fantastic. It's encouraged.

There are women now that teach women to swim. Not just Muslim women, women in general. There are women that purchase the *Burqini* because of health reasons. Doctors and medical practitioners tell them to go and purchase this *Burqini*: "You've got to do certain laps or walk to the pool." So, there are health, weight, and fitness reasons.

There are work reasons. Actually, it's a job for them. We've created jobs. They're learning how to swim, from a very young age, so they're not going to be a mum who can't swim. They're going to teach their kids as well. Honeymooners are having a great time. I went to Malaysia because the Minister of Tourism wanted to personally thank me as it increased tourism within their country.

There are beach parties. There's fun and socializing, for kids and teenagers. There's freedom. There's confidence. There are more women being active. I really, truly, believe that it's got to do with their well-being. Their fitness is all part of well-being, and you're better in your mind, your body and soul, and it's all connected somehow. Was I involved in that? Was I not? Whatever the case was, something has happened. A major thing has happened.

You know what else? Modesty is not a rude word anymore. It used to be. I remember when I was interviewed by journalists and I used to say, "I'm going to say the rude word now. Are you going to sit down? Sit down, be careful, take a deep breath. I produce *modest swimwear*." It's not a rude word anymore. Like, you can actually say it now without cringing: "Modesty!" When I say it out loud, I've got tears in my eyes, like I feel like I'm going to choke. I'm not trying to show off in any way, but it really has made a massive difference—a massive difference.

Anyway, it has been a wonderful journey for all. I think the people that have benefited most are women—women in general. It wasn't me. It was a lot of hard work. Even though it benefited a lot of people, from the moment I started, all I ever did was fight—fight for the defense of rights.

Even though it benefited a lot of people, from the moment I started, all I ever did was fight—fight for the defense of rights.

It's so much bigger than one garment, isn't it?
Yes, it is. It is so much bigger than that. I had no idea. When I say it changed a lot, did it change the world? It changed the world that wanted to change, and it has increased a lot of confidence.

For anyone that wanted to understand about Islam, it sort of assured them. It helped a lot of people who really disliked us through the media to actually understand a little bit more of us. After September 11, they only saw one side. What they saw was just terrorists, evil people. So when the *Burqini* came out with positivity, it gathered up interest. "Hey, I thought Muslim women were terrorists. Why do they want to swim?" And then *Ahiida* came up. And I'm a 4′9″ typical woman, so easy, and like, "Get over it." Somehow, I think it changed a lot of people's attitudes.

I really don't know, but I was very approachable. I was approached by people who hated Muslims. They probably never met another Muslim in their life, so they wanted to let out some steam. I responded to some of them: "Is there something I've done to you, personally?" "Why are you angry with me?" Some of them I just don't bother with. Then you'll get women and people who are curious, "What is it that you really believe in?"

I have always been a very approachable person for anyone that wanted to understand about Islam, but it wasn't what I was trying to do. What I was trying to do is just bring out a product that was going to positively increase your lifestyle. It didn't matter, really, if you were Muslim or not, but it just showed you how people out there probably didn't know a Muslim except me.

You'll always get some people out there that you can't change. They won't. They just refuse to, but I think it had a positive effect in a lot of ways. Who would have thought, a piece of clothing? That just attacks the heart a lot more. It's a personal thing. Clothing is an identity. You get women out there that want to wear a bikini sometimes, or a *Burqini*. I find that clothing is quite personal. It really does bring out who you are. It doesn't matter if you are totally covered or not covered. It's still who you are. You're trying to show, or describe, or talk without actually saying any words about it.

I would love to continue my sports line. When it started, there were no women or girls playing sport. It was a real struggle. It was easier to get them into a *Burqini*, a swimsuit, than a sports garment. So, I would love to continue with that. We've still got another billion people to serve. It continues to completely keep me busy. We'll see how we go. . . .

Fehr Trade

Melissa Fehr (she/her/hers)

London, United Kingdom
http://shop.fehrtrade.com

Melissa Fehr is the founder of *Fehr Trade,* a London-based company providing unique digital sewing patterns for a wide range of sport and activewear. She is also a marathon runner, cyclist, and climber. Melissa started making her own activewear because she struggled to find functional clothing that would also fit well. She believes that anyone can be active, and she wants to empower people to feel comfortable moving their bodies in designs that are fit for purpose and also stylish. Taking a do-it-yourself (DIY) approach, Melissa's patterns encourage people to take matters into their own hands to explore the potential of what they can do through the movement of their bodies.

What encouraged you to start designing your own activewear?

After I was made redundant from my tech job in 2013, I felt I wanted to try something new. I'd been making my own activewear for a while and coming from a tech background meant digital activewear sewing patterns seemed a natural place for me to go. It was also obvious that there were a few nice, basic, activewear patterns out there at the time, but there was a huge opportunity to create patterns with great design lines that looked very fashionable and functional too. There's another subset of patterns that look "sporty" but that don't actually work when you're moving or sweating! So, it was important for me that I road-test every single pattern I create, and I'm proud to say I've run all seven of my marathons in self-sewn gear.

What in your opinion is wrong or missing in activewear available to buy on the high street?

For a start, the fit of ready-to-wear (RTW) activewear is designed to fit the most number of people the least badly. So, it ends up fitting no one body shape perfectly, whether that's a wrong hip-to-waist ratio requiring a drawstring to fix, or constantly having lengths that are too short or too long, requiring constant tugging to stay in place. Then there's the fabrics, which are often so thin when stretched around the body that they're actually see-through. A distinct lack of pockets in the size and placement needed is another problem, not just with activewear but in womenswear in general. So there are quite a few things, but thankfully they're all fairly straightforward to fix when you sew your own activewear!

What do your patterns do? What are they for?

I design patterns for a wide range of activities and sports, like running, cycling, yoga, Pilates, climbing, equestrian riding, weightlifting, and I've even got a tri-suit pattern [a triathlon suit, one-piece garment, designed for swimming, running, and cycling]. Beyond the patterns, I also explain in my Sew Your Own Activewear book how to adapt patterns for basically any activity you can think of—how to break down your movements, to think about the range of motion, repetition, and environment needed and design your adaptations from there. The great thing about sewing your own is that you can get a completely personalized garment, no matter what your body shape or activity. Once you crack the alterations needed, there's no limit to how many garments you can have either, as they're completely repeatable actions.

The great thing about sewing your own is that you can get a completely personalized garment, no matter what your body shape or activity.

As a user of my patterns, I want to forget that I'm wearing anything. I don't want things to be riding up, or chafing, or twisting around, or not have the range of movement that I need for that given activity. Functional, to me, means breaking down the shapes that your body makes, and how often they're doing it, in a way that you can apply to the clothing that you're making. So, you can make clothing that's, overall, pretty good for all activities. But I think, if you want to make something that's absolutely optimal, you can't separate the garment design from the movement, activity or sport that you're going to be doing. You've got to narrow in on exactly what you're going to wear it for.

I say chosen "activity" because it may not even be a sport. It may be just like a movement that you're doing, like a teacher reaching up on the chalkboard. That's a movement and you can actually adapt your patterns for that. So, I break it down into thinking about the environment you are in. That will affect the kind of layers or fabrics that you're choosing. What kind of repetition? What are your limbs doing?

People assume that "your body is your body" and "my arm is this length" and "it's always that length." It's not. It's not always that length. Your skin is really stretchy and if you're trying to do activewear in nonstretchy fabrics for that close fit, it's a losing battle.

How are you rethinking ideas about "active bodies" in your DIY activewear?
We've got to get rid of those old notions of what it means to be active and what it means to be exercising. "If you have a body, you can exercise" is really key to me. I want to bring the idea of empowerment to everyone, even if they think that they're not active.

We've got to get rid of those old notions of what it means to be active and what it means to be exercising. "If you have a body, you can exercise."

Everybody has got some sort of movement, or some sort of activity or exercise that is for them, that they will actually enjoy. If people say, "No, I don't exercise. I just x,y,z." I'm like, "x,y,z is exercise. You're just not thinking of it that way." I think it's an identity thing.

Sewing your own clothing is so good for your own body image and getting away from your size being a number. You can mix and match between different sizes, or draft your own, and change it up. I haven't the foggiest idea what size these jeans are [points at trousers she is wearing]. I honestly don't. I've made them so many times it's just a "me" pattern.

If I go to a shop now, I would have to take about five sizes to the changing room because I literally don't know what size I am anymore. I am more interested in what my body can do, not what my body looks like. That is a huge step in terms of body positivity.

You include a lot of pockets in your patterns and talk about them often in your books. What's so important about pockets for activewear?
Everybody wants pockets. I think this might be the single biggest factor that gets people sewing their own activewear. People just want more, and more,

Figure 2.3
Melissa in her sewing room wearing a *Sweat Luxe* top.
Credit: Melissa Fehr / *Fehr Trade*

and more pockets. There are some really good places to put pockets, and some really bad ones. For runners, hips and backs are really good places. Your stomach or underneath your arm are really bad spots because your arms are going to be moving and hitting against that. People want them in the right place, that aren't going to be jumping around. They want pockets that are big enough for their phone. I've actually had to redevelop several of my patterns because phones have gotten so much bigger.

A lot of people want to have a few items on them at all times. People want to be self-sufficient. It was the start of London Marathon—I think it

Figure 2.4
Melissa running the London Marathon 2019 in *Sew Your Own Activewear* Active Leggings.
Credit: Melissa Fehr / *Fehr Trade*

was 2019—I got talking to these ladies who were next to me and they were like, "Have you got a business card?" I'd love to make your patterns. It was the pockets. "Oh, my god, you have what, six pockets here?" and I was like, "Yes, I've got a lot of gels." But I'm running a marathon. I don't carry a business card with me to run a marathon. "You're just going to have to remember the name of my pattern company."

Why are you encouraging people to make their own versions?

If people sew, I'm giving them not only the ability to make that garment in exactly the way that they want that works for them, but also the skill to say, "I could make changes." This empowers people to think about their own activewear and to make it their own, rather than just buying something and saying, "I'd really like this if it wasn't for this one thing," "I really like this, but it doesn't come in my size," and "Actually, yes, this is a nice design, but it'd be even better if . . ." and then they start mashing them together. I love it when people "franken-pattern."

A franken-pattern is an unofficial sewing term for combining several existing patterns together into one garment. So, you might take the sleeves from one pattern, the upper body from another, and the lower body from a third, plus a particular pocket from a fourth. This level of customization is impossible when buying garments but straightforward when you sew your own.

Exercising is really empowering for just about everyone. If you add in that other layer of, like, "Yes, I made this myself," that just elevates it a bit.

Ride With Wolves

Ester Van Kempen (she/her/hers)

Utrecht, Netherlands and London, United Kingdom

Dutch designer Ester Van Kempen is the founder of *Ride With Wolves*, an inclusive brand based in Utrecht and London. The *Ride With Wolves* line of cycling wearables, with retro-reflective elements, is designed for any gender and all body types. Although made for everyday cycling, items are also intended to be worn while off the bike. What is unique about the collection is its striking response to urban harassment. Ester talks about the injury caused by catcalling and verbal abuse and how it shapes the experience of public space for many women and marginalized people. *Ride With Wolves* aims to transform this one-way abuse into empowering dialogue by reflecting responses in high-visibility ink. By (literally) highlighting the issue, Ester aims to open up both conversation and public space to a greater diversity of road users.

How did *Ride With Wolves* begin?

Ride With Wolves came out of a different clothing brand called *House of Astbury*, which was a very grassroots brand I set up with two of my friends at the time, Monika Zamojska and Ren Aldridge. We all went our own ways and I decided to continue as *Ride With Wolves*. It had the same concept, but I rebranded it and went a bit more commercial. We used a lot of slogans like "Thunder Thighs" and "Cats Against Cat Calling," with *House of Astbury*, which are fantastic and I still love them, but I took that a step further.

Initially with *House of Astbury*, we felt that there was not enough reflective clothing for women or for younger people to be able to afford. We could find cheaper wear, but it didn't feel like us. We are quite punk and alternative, so that's when we decided, "Why can't we do it ourselves? What makes a product a cycle product?" So, we looked at what kind of things are out there, what's missing, and how you can, with the patches, for example, upgrade your own clothing with a reflective element that feels safer on the road.

We felt uncomfortable wearing tight Lycra clothing, especially off our bikes, because it's very body-shaping and you are then labeled as a "cyclist."

Figure 2.5
Ride With Wolves–*Wolves against wolf whistling 2017*.
Credit: *Ride With Wolves* / Photo: Owen Richards

We just wanted something that you feel cool and comfortable in on and off your bike.

So, we found reflective ink and began screen-printing. We started with small products like patches that you sew onto clothing. Then we began working on other products like leggings, bags, and sweaters, and made it into a collection.

What's behind the name *Ride With Wolves*?
Ride With Wolves is loosely based on a feminist book about women who run with wolves, being part of a pack.[10] When they look at each other and when they see each other, they understand the struggles they've been through, the aims they have, the goals they have, and, like, where they are at in life.

Cycling in London specifically looks like it's very much about the skinny men in Lycra on fast racing bikes. When we started cycling you would barely see any other women, or people of different body sizes, so by not seeing them, there weren't any role models. You need to have a role model to feel like you can cycle as well.

You need to have a role model to feel like you can cycle as well.

I feel part of a pack when I see a different female cyclist or just cyclists in general. You just look at each other briefly and you're like, "Yes, we get each other." Especially in London, less so in the Netherlands because everyone cycles, but there's something about when you're going fast and you're in your zone and then you see this other cyclist and you feel this euphoria of "Yes, this is what we're about." I started seeing my own clothes in London on other cyclists, and I even organized events for people to buy the clothes and screen-print their clothes themselves. You feel part of that pack. You feel a bond between each other. I think that is something really important to me.

What are some of the key issues in cycling that you set out to address?
Monika worked in the cycling industry, in bike shops, and found it was very male dominated. She kept coming home with all kinds of stories about how she wouldn't be able to get a job as a bike mechanic because she's a woman. It's also about cycling in London and being cat-called, being dragged off our bikes, getting slapped on our bums, experiencing horrific sexist stuff, and no one was really there to listen to it. So, we were just like, "You know what? We're just going to be really blunt and we're going to put this on our clothes," and we'll make it reflective, so it lights up.

We started doing all the big cycle events. We went to the Cycle London events and others to create a voice and just be a group of women on the bill, because all the big bike brands were primarily made up of men. I really feel like it has changed in the last few years, I see a lot more women there, but when we started it was really unique.

Can you talk more about your unique approach to urban harassment?
Harassment is a very negative experience, but so many people, especially women, experience it. Because of that, it can also be a bonding and

Figure 2.6
Ride With Wolves 2016.
Credit: *Ride With Wolves* / Photo: Owen Richards

empowering experience when it's shared. When we started talking about these experiences as a group of friends and at events we organized, more people started coming forward. We were also able to debunk that negative experience because we could grow from each other's experiences.

I think *House of Astbury* and *Ride With Wolves* were a way of taking back that strength, because when you get harassed, you kind of lose a bit of yourself, you suddenly feel very small and you're scared, and by doing that project, by doing this clothing line, it really felt like we were taking back the power and our own energies.

Ride With Wolves was a way of taking back that strength, because when you get harassed, you kind of lose a bit of yourself, you suddenly feel very small and you're scared, and by doing that project, by doing this clothing line, it really felt like we were taking back the power and our own energies.

We want to say, "You should feel safer, but you're not going to, per se, be safer." It's about being more visible, but at the same time it's not really about that. We were more interested in generating different kinds of visibility— visibility in the cycling industry and on the street. Making those statements was more important than conventional safety visibility.

What are you bringing to the cycling world?
I guess it's just about kicking against establishments. The three of us came from a punk house and grew up with the punk community, so we had that as a life-style. It is just the way we do things. And we had nothing to lose by going into the cycling industry. We felt like no one was really listening. From Monika's stories in the cycling industry and working in bike shops, they weren't really hearing her. Even our male friends didn't really hear us. So, we were like, "We just need to open a conversation in a whole different way." Reading these slo-gans they might still say "Well, we don't need it," or, "Isn't that a bit harsh?" or, like "Not all men," or whatever, but it just has to be said to start a conversation. We were just like, "Well, fuck it, let's just go for it. We have nothing to lose."

Petticoat Dress and Urban Blanket

Nicolas Moser (he/him/his)

Geneva, Switzerland and Hanoi, Vietnam
https://www.multiplyoffice.com

Nicolas Moser leads a team of architects, urban planners, researchers, and designers at *Multiply Office* in Hanoi and Geneva. Collectively they apply multidisciplinary skills and interests to address social and political issues, question encroachments on public space, and experiment with experiences in different surroundings. We talk with Nicolas about two projects: *Petticoat Dress* and *Urban Blanket*. One explores people's ability to extend private living into public space, and the other emerged in relation to spatial restrictions shaped by COVID-19. Both reflect on the challenges of claiming public space as pedestrians, the delight of unexpected encounters, and the potential of mundane acts of resistance.

How do your architecture and design practices combine with your interest in cities and civic space?

I've been an architect for many years and I am fascinated by people and cities. Multiply Office does objects, furniture, architecture, and urban planning. We approach every project as an opportunity to better understand what is happening around us and how we can be part of it. And, maybe, help people understand that they can also be part of it. We infer that from architecture and urban planning design, but we use different ingredients according to which subject we're working on.

We opened the studio in January 2020, and we are working between Switzerland and Vietnam. I came to Hanoi fifteen years ago to open one of the branches of a Swiss company where I was working and I never left. Here we have opportunities to make and test things, to make prototypes. We can see a lot of things changing very fast. There are a lot of new things: both traditional and contemporary. The city is kind of an interesting laboratory.

Sometimes we feel that people are too passive or that they feel it is not their place to make decisions or even just participate in something. We try to question that. We try to see things differently by approaching it from another angle. You can see an object ten times and it is always the same. But suddenly something happens, and you see it differently. It loses its primary function, and it becomes something new, something else. We are very interested in this moment, when something becomes new.

We try to play with scale and we question the meaning of things. Our motto could be, "Let's be part of the city, let's use things around us." In the same way that we need to recycle, we try to be inventive and innovative in the way we use things. We adjust things to show that change is possible. If we are not satisfied with something, if we think we don't have the things we need, we don't go buy a new one. First we look around at things we actually have. Maybe we have them already. Maybe we just need to redesign them (give them a makeover) or use them differently.

In the same way that we need to recycle, we try to be inventive and innovative in the way we use things. We adjust things to show that change is possible.

What made you, as an architect, venture into working with wearables—such as with the projects *Urban Blanket* and *Petticoat Dress*?

I think my interest in architecture and in clothing is quite basic: we live in houses and we have clothes and fabric around us. I like the city. I like to be outside and meet people. And I also don't like very many constraints. So, I consider our *Urban Blanket* as the one tool you can always have with you: around your neck or in your bag ready to be used. You don't know what will happen today, right? Maybe you go to a picnic. Maybe you want to take a nap, or read a book under a tree. Maybe you want to go outside but you are a bit cold. Maybe you go to the beach. It is like being a kid, being ready for anything the day will offer to you, without needing to plan ahead. For me this is how the city and architecture match together. It's something very easy to do. The *Urban Blanket* could not be simpler. It's a piece of fabric 1.5 meters by 1.5 meters. You can use any fabric. It doesn't need to be designed.

The *Petticoat Dress* happened at the beginning of the pandemic but it was quite similar: answering a need with a simple tool. We were thinking: "Okay, we have this problem. Now we have to find a solution to keep going. What can we imagine [we need] to go outside?" We knew that it was difficult to keep a distance from other people in public space. And it was also difficult to remember to do so all the time. Then we had this idea. You want to go to a festival, but you cannot because you'll be packed together? Let's put something on to maintain space between each other. So, we designed the *Petticoat Dress*. At first it was only a 2D image that we posted on Instagram. A lot of people, from at least twenty different countries, contacted us and asked for information and to publish it. It was very surprising. So we tried to make it real.

This was the first time we solved a problem in terms of clothing. In architecture, we know how to deal with details. We thought we were good at sewing

Figure 2.7
Urban Blanket project, Hong Kong 2019.
Credit: *Multiply Office* / Photo: Joseph Gobin

things but then we started to work with fashion designers. It was very interesting to learn and discover fashion things. Until then, we were very proud of the mock-up dress, but talking with them made us realize that our design was really simple in terms of details. We became a bit embarrassed of our work, because you cannot present it as a piece of clothing, if it doesn't work as one.

We made a few prototypes. Some were very easy and others super difficult, more like artisanal pieces. When we did the photo shoot, there were five or six dresses. It was interesting because then we understood the design a little bit more than when we just had the image. It was clothing. We were inside something. We felt many things while wearing the dress. For example, when you get too close, the dresses touch each other. It shapes how you move. You feel super light, you can feel the wind and there is movement.

How do your projects create private and personal space for people in public?
It's kind of a democratic process. It's very interesting. When you're on the street, you can sit on the street or on the pavement. But as soon as you put out the blanket and you sit on it, you define a border, your own personal space. You feel more comfortable because you are not just sitting in the middle of the street anymore. You are arranging the city —having a bit of your own corner of it.

You feel more comfortable because you are not just sitting in the middle of the street anymore. You are arranging the city —having a bit of your own corner of it.

You do not want to sit on the street because it's dirty? Use the *Urban Blanket*! It encourages people to do things they haven't planned. You want to go to the park? You have the blanket. You don't want to get wet? You have the blanket to cover yourself. It allows you to not have everything planned out to do something. It's very small and very cheap. It is something everybody can have. Just go picnic on the street. You have the city, and the city can bring you so many opportunities. And it can be our blanket or any kind of blanket.

In the *Petticoat Dress*, you have your own space. The edges around you are very clear. When people are moving or walking, it is very similar to a ballet, a choreography. You need to look at what is around you, but you can touch people, and it's a bit soft. It was funny when we did the photo shoot. We asked friends but they didn't know each other. [In the dress] we touch each other a little less aggressively than if we touch each other with our hands. It was really an extension of yourself.

Also, because you feel the weight, you feel the space and you feel this physical distance. It was a very interesting piece of clothing to wear. We had to learn how to move with the dress, to understand how this piece of clothing works. If you run too fast, you have problems. At the beginning, it was very impractical and then step by step you get used to it. Even going through doors: you have to wait and look at the other person. You have to have an interaction with each other to avoid problems. It becomes a new opportunity and an elegant way to interact with others. You are not scared anymore because you know you will stay two meters apart. You are protected. You just have to learn how to wear it. We did a movie, like a

Figure 2.8
Petticoat Dress, Hanoi 2020.
Credit: *Multiply Office* / Photo: Cedric Florentin

Figure 2.9
Petticoat Dress, Kaunas 2022.
Credit: *Multiply Office* / Photo: Martynas Plepys

manual, to show how it works. It allowed us to understand what was not instinctive in the beginning.

Who did you design it for?
Initially it was not designed as a skirt for women. It was not gendered. We took reference from men's kilts. We looked at its design to understand how to make our dress. So for us, all could wear our *Petticoat Dress*. We also added some features to make it more or less gendered. For example, you have a button on the side a bit like trousers. Or you can have the zipper on the back a bit more like a dress. And now we have this system that you can put it in a bag and then pull it out quite fast. You can take it everywhere with you. You can carry it on your bicycle, when you get to a destination you put it on and can enjoy yourself.

How do you want people to feel in your designs?
Free. I believe that with the dress or with the blanket, you have more opportunity to do things. It's not only for yourself. The size of the blanket is good for two or three people. The dress is a bit different, but you can imagine that

you can go and see your grandmother because you're not afraid anymore. You protect her as well. Our designs are a message, a form of public engagement, a claim that we are part of the society. You take a position on something, which is quite important. You take the responsibility of it, you don't hide. It's the point actually: you can't, you shouldn't hide. I think that's important.

Our designs are a message, a form of public engagement, a claim that we are part of the society.

3 CONCEALING

While citizens have always watched and been watched by others, the ubiquity and pervasiveness of digital technologies now subjects us to even more surveillance and amplifies the need for privacy. According to sociologist James Rule, privacy is "the ability of individuals to control the flow of information about themselves—even in the face of others' demands for access to such information."[1] Without this ability, as surveillance studies scholars note, the consequences can be wide ranging and impact many parts of daily life. David Lyon draws attention to the power of "surveillance as social sorting," which shapes everything from what kinds of online deals we get offered to how we are treated at airports.[2] Simone Browne writes about "racializing surveillance" as a "technology of social control," which often results in "discriminatory treatment."[3] And, as Rachel Dubrofsky and Shoshana Magnet argue, the gendered, racialized, sexualized, and classed dimensions of surveillance show how "supposedly 'neutral' technologies" can "intensify existing inequalities."[4] Fundamentally, surveillance and the lack of privacy play key roles in how people behave and are treated, where they live, work, and how they dwell in and move through public space.

Of course, our privacy is not always forcibly taken without consent. Many of us willingly carry tracking devices in the form of mobile phones and loyalty cards. These technologies constantly record our data, which we offer to the state and corporations in exchange for goods and services, rights, and protections. This is not new. Ideas around transparency and visibility have always mapped onto citizenship. Being a citizen involves giving up information, often with little assurance of its resulting use, misuse, or distribution (such as applying for citizenship). Openness and transparency are seen as central to being a "good citizen." After all, as the familiar saying goes, "If you've got nothing to hide, you've got nothing to fear." Yet, we all need privacy and the freedom to keep some things concealed or secret. In fact, the right to privacy and a private life is enshrined in law in the Universal Declaration of Human Rights and the European Convention of Human Rights.[5]

For many, however, it is difficult, if not sometimes impossible, to resist being monitored or caught up in webs of surveillance. This is because surveillance manifests in many forms, originating from intimate sources, such as friends and family, or strangers on social media, while others are initiated by large-scale and anonymous organizations. However, while surveillance can limit an individual's freedoms, it can also catalyze activism through defiance. In some contexts, resisting constant surveillance by keeping even small, modest, or mundane things private can be examined as an act of resistance. There are many examples of wearables being used to resist invasive pressures and provide alternative experiences of the world.

This chapter explores wearables that help to conceal something. To conceal is to "prevent (something) from being known," "to keep secret" or to "hide."[6] As Shahidha Bari evocatively writes, "Clothes can be the disguise in which we dissolve, the camouflage that allows us to keep something of ourselves in reserve, as though the only thing we are and own is that which we refuse to articulate in our outerwear."[7] Pockets, for instance, according to dress historians Barbara Burman and Ariane Fenneatux, might be small and mundane but they have long provided the means for people, particularly women, to secure personal goods and maintain precious private space at times when they have been denied both.[8] Exploring wearables as acts and performances of concealment has the potential to unsettle assumptions built into the corporeal normativity of citizenship and public space.

The following wearables are used to creatively resist dominant and conventional forces of surveillance in public space. Designers are motivated by a range of privacy issues, including digital freedoms, spatial politics, and gender expression. They make use of mundane and ordinary things—coats, bandanas, chest binders, and makeup—to experiment with alternative ways to inhabit public (data) spaces. These designs invite us to look beyond the idea of transparency being central to normative "good citizens" by keeping something deliberately hidden, thereby evading the ever-watchful gaze. These designs do more than "merely trick the monitoring program in question," as John Gilliom and Torin Monahan write, they "offer a broader ideological challenge to the forced visibility that is central to surveillance societies."[9]

We start with an example of digital resistance. **Leon Baauw** discusses anti-surveillance coats that he developed with collaborator Marcha Schagen for **Project KOVR**. Wearing these designs provide citizens with confidence that their data and digital identities remain safe. The coats also offer the experience of being "disconnected" in locations with high levels of networked surveillance. "One of the hardest things to explain to people," Leon admits, is "that something invisible might actually . . . pose a threat." The challenge was how to raise the profile of the problem they were addressing—"to make the invisible visible." The designers of *Project KOVR* are not against digital technology, but rather they want wearers to have more choices about where and when they give away their data in public space: "Let's try to humanize technology and make sure that we can still remain human in a way, by being able to switch off in any way possible."

Protesters are often rightfully cautious about surveillance systems, particularly highly monitored communications networks in particular places. **Xuedi Chen** and **Pedro Oliveira,** designers of the **Backslash** kit, identified that the needs of citizens taking to the streets to protest their rights included being able to organize and to adapt to changing conditions: "Lots of new authoritarian tech was being used against people in the streets, and governments were shutting down communications." *Backslash* uses wearables as the medium to protect bodies and send messages. For example, the *Backslash* kit includes a smart bandana with coded print. Xuedi and Pedro explain, "The bandana has a pattern that, depending on how you fold it, can send different messages." Although these designs are useful, the designers' primary aim is to share ideas and discuss issues: "In our case, the real disruption, or the real disobedience, is to talk about protests."

Some public spaces place citizens under forms of surveillance that are less visible than others. **Emily Roderick** and **Georgina Rowlands** are members of *The Dazzle Club*, a group that runs arts-based walks in densely populated, highly surveilled areas of London such as Kings Cross and Canary Wharf. Our interview with Emily and Georgina elicits a very different perspective on wearables—by considering the subject through the lens of makeup. They use Computer Vision Dazzle (CV Dazzle), a technique inspired by the attention-grabbing dazzle camouflage that was used in World Wars I and II not to hide battleships but to obscure information about their shape, speed, and direction. In a strategy analogous to this, *The Dazzle Club* uses CV Dazzle to draw attention to, and resist, facial recognition technology by painting faces with bold geometric shapes that cannot be read and stored by digital machines.

The high visibility of this makeup contrasts with the ubiquitous invisible technologies that we cannot see working (and therefore have fewer cues to reject). *The Dazzle Club*'s public walks question who has the right to privacy in public spaces. As Emily and Georgina explain, "We are actively trying to opt out of being recognized by facial recognition. We're trying to resist the passiveness of being a person walking around public space and being analyzed, and having our data harvested and our biometric data read."

A different perspective on concealment in public space is provided by humanwear artist **Sissel Kärneskog**. They recognize the familiarity and safety that comes with conventional dressing and performing "normal" in public. Sissel's design practice sets out to claim safety while decentering the normalizing power of andronormativity and binary gender identities. They explain, "Being queer, a lot of spaces are extremely intimidating to be in. So, you don't know, wherever you go in the world, if you're going to meet an ally or someone who is against you. It can be really intimidating to just be clear about who you are." Sissel approaches wearables as "costumes" that enable wearers to subvert normative roles and play with power relations. Reworking recognizable forms, such as classic suits, into "nearly normal" wearables enables Sissel to "hack the system" and experiment with other ways of being in social situations.

By reframing everyday objects and seemingly ordinary interactions, these designers raise important questions about things we take for granted. Their designs aid wearers in a range of diverse and creative ways to resist the ubiquity of an ever-watchful gaze, in all its forms, by keeping something hidden or cleverly coded. So, while in some ways wearables can reveal a lot about wearers, it's also the case that they can cleverly cover up and conceal.

Project KOVR

Leon Baauw (he/him/his)

Rotterdam, Netherlands
https://projectkovr.com

Project KOVR [pronounced "cover"] is a wearable countermovement developed by Dutch designers Leon Baauw and Marcha Schagen. Together they research and design wearables that protect people's digital privacy in places with high surveillance technologies. Playing on ideas about in/visibility, their shiny reflective coats and accessories are an attempt to give people (back) a choice about when and how they might be traced when moving through public space. Made of metalliferous fabrics, their designs are essentially wearable Faraday cages that block ingoing and outgoing electromagnetic signals. In light of seemingly ongoing data scandals, *Project KOVR* works to raise awareness about data security and citizens' rights to privacy.

How does your interest in privacy intersect with wearables?

That's exactly what my teachers at art school asked: "Why is a graphic designer making clothing?" And I think, in short, it was really about creating something that was easy to use and easy to understand for a large audience. We started looking into these different surveillance systems; the ways we were being monitored both online as well as offline when you walk around in the streets. In Rotterdam, for example, we have trams that record conversations and facial recognition. All these kinds of different systems sparked my interest and as an artist I really wanted to warn people about it first, so that was really my approach—to warn people.

"This is not okay."

"You should protect your privacy."

So that was the main reason I started making different critiques. Different designs were always critiques. At a certain point I figured, "Why not try to make something that creates awareness and also make sure that people can actually use it?."

I started thinking, well, we all have clothing. We wear clothing. It's pretty normal. Why not make clothing that can protect you against the modern threats of our society. Clothing has always protected us against the cold. Clothing even protects us against other extremes like heat, for instance. Firefighters and race car drivers need protective suits against extreme heat. And clothing has always protected us against the threats of the biosphere. Why not design and make something that can protect you against the new challenges that we have around? So that is basically the idea behind why I started making clothing and I had never made anything. I'm not a fashion designer. I'm a graphic designer. So, I worked with Marcha to find out whether it was even possible to create a functional prototype. I think the idea started in 2014 or 2015 and we had our first prototype in 2016.

At that point we created a snowball. Before we knew it, we were on Dutch national television and then it just started to get bigger and bigger. It was also in a period where people still had this idea that if you have something to hide, you must be a terrorist or criminal.

I think public opinion has changed and people now see our design as something that is very logical. The data scandals in regard to Facebook and others changed public opinion. I think we surfed on that wave in a way. We also got requests to produce them in larger quantities.

When we first made it, we really had to explain because people kept asking us: "What is wrong with companies following you?" and "Why are you so paranoid about all these different systems?" It's so interesting to see how this has changed in just a few years. The project really shows that as well. It was based on something negative, but we turned it into something positive.

Why is a coat such a productive medium to translate these ideas?
I probably have a different view towards clothing than perhaps a fashion designer would. But I like how putting on a coat is like adding an extra layer to protect yourself against cold or even heat. So, I really like that metaphor of putting on clothing, a coat, for example, to actually protect yourself against what is out there and I use it for a digital theme. But the idea also needs to work. So that was phase two. We had to do a lot of different testing and material research just to see if we could also make a working prototype and eventually we succeeded. So that was a win for us.

Figure 3.1
Anti-Surveillance Coat Type I (2016).
Credit: *Project KOVR* / Photo: Suzanne Waijers

We created a wearable working prototype and that was something I didn't really expect. In the beginning I was focused on the metaphor itself, and thinking perhaps it was something that could be done in the future. But we actually made it work quite easily.

Your website talks about "counter wearable movements"—can you explain a bit more about this?
We had an activist mindset when we started the project. We wanted to give people tools to regain their privacy. And because your privacy has already been at risk for a while, there's not much you could do. These days a lot more is possible. For example, Apple released a new operating system in which you can choose whether you want to be followed by certain apps or not. That wasn't possible back then. Everything was always on. You were always being followed. That was the norm or becoming the norm and we really wanted to use this activist language to hype people up, to create a certain urgency and create activists.

How hard is it to communicate urgent ideas around an issue that's largely invisible?

It was one of the hardest things to explain to people—that something invisible might actually scan you or pose a threat. So that has also always been a challenge for us—to make the invisible visible. And there's also a bit of a paradox in there, of course. The title of my graduate thesis was "Being Visible by Wanting to Be Invisible." Because at that time, if you weren't on Facebook, if you said you cared about privacy, you stood out. You had something to hide or you were probably a criminal or terrorist. You had bad intentions.

I like the fact that the fabric that we found worked and has a reflective side of it. So, in every light it looks a bit different. It reflects whatever lights fall onto it. It's difficult to protect yourself against something that is invisible but the fabric itself was reflective. I think in a way, that was our answer to the invisible thing that was out there, that was looking at you.

One of the ideas behind the project was to change that way of thinking. Making the coats really stand out from normal clothing was part of playing with that paradox. We chose to have the reflective fabric on the outside of the coat, instead of putting it in the inside. Because if we put in on the inside, it would be just like any other coat.

Who are you designing for?

Everyone. Our idea was to create something that might be needed in the future. We hoped it wouldn't be necessary. But it became relevant the moment we created the prototype. Our idea was to create something that was almost like a dystopian idea, like: "Let's not go where we need clothing like this." But when our prototype was available, it was already a necessity.

We started selling some of our coats. We sold them to art collectors and to museums. We also sold one to someone in Hong Kong, which I thought was really necessary because they were using all kinds of weird technological methods to do facial recognition and to scan the phones of protesters. Perhaps in the future it will be normal to have a layer of this material in your clothing. I know that in military-grade clothing, this material is used. Perhaps we will have a certain backpack or laptop sleeve, or coat or whatever,

Figure 3.2
Anti-Surveillance Coat Type II (2017).
Credit: *Project KOVR* / Photo: Suzanne Waijers

that has a layer of this material inside of it because it protects you and your body from radiation and other possible threats.

I have a wallet, for instance, that has this material inside it. It has become pretty normal to find all kinds of products to shield your devices. And it's also used in phone covers and backpacks. So, in a way, it's already here.

I still really hope that we can progress to a world in which we are able to switch off. Let's not go towards a completely transparent society in which everything you do, everything you say, everything you've ever done is being either recorded, scanned, or saved. Let's go to a society that moves towards technology where you can switch off and log on when you want to.

I still really hope that we can progress to a world in which we are able to switch off.

I'm not against technology at all. I think technology is fascinating, but let's try to humanize technology. Let's make sure that we can still remain human by being able to switch off. We are starting to create a world, or perhaps we've already created it, in which you cannot just log off anymore. From the moment you were born, you were already being followed or monitored.

Do you think your designs make wearers behave differently?
That's a good question. When we started this project and we had the first interviews, a lot of people were asking me if I'd created the perfect coat for terrorists or if I'd made a backpack that can be used by thieves. I think in a way, you do feel a bit more safe. It's like browsing with a VPN [Virtual Private Network] so you know you're not being monitored directly, but I think it also has a moral aspect. If you want to do something, if you have bad intentions, then I don't really think our clothing is going to be the ultimate factor that decides whether you will go stealing or do something even worse.

I think that's also being human: to just do stupid stuff every now and then. So, I think I can't really answer the question directly because it's also just how you are as a person and what your intentions and motives are and how you're being raised in the country you live in. And if you want to do something bad, if you have bad intentions, then there are all kinds of methods to stay hidden. I don't think our clothing is either creating more criminals or people with bad intentions.

I really enjoy the fact that we're bringing a message. I'm also completely fine with people disagreeing with me. I just want people to start thinking about it more, perhaps create more awareness or let people form their own opinions. When we started this project, a lot of people never really thought about it. It wasn't until these giant data scandals and the manipulation of the US elections and other kinds of big topics that people started thinking about it more. It was always one of our goals to create more awareness and to have this design be a catalyst for opinions and for debate.

It was always one of our goals to create more awareness and to have this design be a catalyst for opinions and for debate.

Backslash

Xuedi Chen (she/her/hers) and Pedro Oliveira (he/him/his)

New York, United States
http://www.backslash.cc

Backslash was developed by New York–based multidisciplinary designers Xuedi Chen and Pedro Oliveira. It is a toolkit of low-cost open-source wearable devices designed for protesters to help them avoid conflict with authorities and to communicate during network blackouts. It prioritizes off-grid communication and includes a bandana that embeds hidden messages in patterns, a wearable panic button, a jammer to reclaim personal smartphone privacy, personal blackbox devices to register law enforcement abuse, and routers for off-grid communication. *Backslash* recognizes that a one-size-fits-all approach is impractical and aims instead to spark debate with provocative design for use by protesters now and in the future.

What is *Backslash* and how did it begin?

Pedro: Backslash started when I moved to New York in 2012. I'm originally from Brazil. In 2013, I went back home to visit and do some work. During this time there was an explosion of protesting in Brazil, especially in São Paulo, where I was based at the time. I was going to those protests and I had some friends who were documenting and taking photos and working for publications or independent NGOs [non-governmental organizations]. It really stuck with me.

We come from a mixed tech and design background. So, we both try to inject our practice with a mixture of design-orientated critical and artistic practice. We went to grad school together at New York University and I met some people from Turkey who had been part of protests and they connected me with others from the Gezi Park protests. I also met people involved in the Occupy protests here in New York. So that's when I started to make connections and began talking to people and exploring how we could translate this into design-based research.

Xuedi: We constructed the *Backslash* kit during a time where there was a wave of protests that included the use of new technologies, especially from authorities and governments. Lots of new authoritarian tech was being used against people in the streets, and governments were shutting down communications. We come from a community of makers who are always thinking about how grassroots movements are being built and how communities can come together to innovate. So, we thought around that in terms of protest culture. We've also been seeing how tech was being used from the protester side and the use of social media, for example, to spread messages and to organize. We really wanted to brainstorm around that and see the different ways that people were able to innovate.

Can you talk about some of the wearables in the *Backslash* kit?

Pedro: The wearable panic button, for example, was specifically designed to address some of the situations that people call kettling. This practice is used by the authorities. They start to close some of the streets to funnel the flow of the protesters to a specific area where they could all be arrested or beaten, and sometimes people get harmed. And we thought it was important, even if they have scenarios that have jammed the cell towers, that people could still be able to know that this was happening and still be able to send some of those messages. People further away from the area could be alerted and think, "Oh,

Figure 3.3
Backslash bandana.
Credit: *Backslash*

maybe I should escape before getting trapped there." They would be able to pinpoint where that was happening so they could avoid those areas.

We came up with the bandana because we saw that some countries which have laws against speaking out against the government were sending people to a lifetime in jail. We wanted to think about how people could communicate outside of the country. For example, how could someone send a message to a journalist. The bandana has a pattern that, depending on how you fold it, can send different messages. If you see it from one side, the pattern shows something, if you fold it in a different way, even though it seems to be exactly the same thing, it's a different pattern. At the time, it allowed us to send up to eight different messages.

The bandana has a pattern that, depending on how you fold it, can send different messages.

Why did you focus on wearables?

Xuedi: We took a scenario-based approach, and many happened to manifest in wearable form. For example, the bandana was seen as a scenario of being able to pass messages inconspicuously, using a hash or a pattern to unlock a message. That was something that we saw translated well into something that you can wear on your body. You can be moving about, and photographs can be taken of you. It serves a dual purpose of covering the face and the pattern can be used as a key to unlock messages.

Pedro: Also, because of the nature of protests, people are moving a lot of the time. Sure, there are some examples, like Occupy, where people are camping. But in many examples, people were moving or marching. We're also trying to highlight the technologies being used against protests. So, the idea is that you needed to be mobile, you needed to be fast, and you needed to have fast deployable tech. It made sense that it needed to be with you. If it's too big for you to carry or if it needs to be stationary, that wouldn't work.

Often during a protest, it is about appropriating what you have in your hands. For example, some people build face shields with plastic bottles. Others have makeshift shields or barricades. So, we thought about how this idea can be translated to electronics and those types of things.

Who is your toolkit designed for?

Pedro: We didn't have a political agenda, and this was not a call for action. This was not an idea to say we are pro-China, pro-Hong Kong, or anything like that. It was really to highlight some of the scenarios, some of the technologies being used against the protesters all over the globe, and show how we could have the conversation and imagine alternative scenarios. We were inspired by different technologies and practices we were researching, but they're not designed for specific countries or specific groups. It was more about: "Oh, what are some patterns we are seeing? And how can we highlight these and have conversations about the use of such technologies by the authorities?"

It was really to highlight some of the scenarios, some of the technologies being used against the protesters all over the globe and show how we could have the conversation and imagine alternative scenarios.

Figure 3.4
Backslash kit.
Credit: *Backslash*

Xuedi: We hope that it's not needed, but we understand that a problem exists. And it's something that we should be talking about. Designing for the near future is a little bit tricky. But the way we're approaching it is by imagining how communities would be able to come together to creatively use different kinds of tech. So, it's not saying, "We want you to imagine whole new tech." But in the future, how can people use their creativity to appropriate and hack to change what we already have and apply it to their immediate needs? It's about really starting the conversation around how communities can leverage their unique resources and use that to innovate for themselves.

So, it's not saying, "We want you to imagine whole new tech." But in the future, how can people use their creativity to appropriate and hack to change what we already have and apply it to their immediate needs?

It's always a cat-and-mouse game with tech. Once you innovate, the authorities will find a way to get around that. It's always about staying nimble and a little bit ahead of them and anticipating what's to come next. So that's why we wanted to frame this research more around the discourse and building community and around being able to innovate. Because this innovation cannot come from one source. It needs to be a decentralized community-based kind of innovation.

Pedro: We're big fans of open-source technologies, and we're big fans of the open-source hardware movement and all that. But putting all the information outside could also play against it. Some people could believe those things were like silver bullets for some kind of scenario and a solution, which could be really harmful. If you put it out there and make every single detail transparent, then you can also have authorities and other people building counter measurements. This is really tricky. We realized during the research that people can really get hurt. If we put all this out there, people could get killed or get sent to jail for life.

Why, in your opinion, is the freedom and ability to protest as a citizen so important?

Pedro: At the time, it was not only about freedom to protest but the belief that communication is a basic human right. It was about communicating and spreading the message locally, but also on a global scale. We understand that if you are tired of not being heard, a protest might be the only way to communicate, to have a voice. And we both agree that communication is a basic human right, but we also think that the freedom of expression, the freedom to protest, is something that should be out there. And we definitely think we should defend that.

We both agree that communication is a basic human right, but we also think that the freedom of expression, the freedom to protest, is something that should be out there.

Xuedi: Many people have responded by saying, "Yeah, this is a very important conversation to have." And from another direction, we also get a lot of requests for manufacturing. "This is the kind of tech we need," "We want to replicate this," and "We have the situation here in this country right now." So, it's clear that it's a meaningful conversation to have and something that people feel is needed. So that very much validates the direction taken with the research.

Are your designs available to buy or are they about sparking larger conversations?

Pedro: We are against this kind of techno-solutionism. People said, "Oh, so how can you mass-produce these? How can you monetize these?" That was not the approach for us. We really wanted to spark the discourse. We understand that protests are different depending on where you're based. We don't think we can build a one-size-fits-all solution. And that was never the idea. The idea was really, "How can we showcase the different scenarios, the different tech that is deployed around protest sites, and how can people understand the larger impact?"

When you see the waves of protest appearing all over the world, you start to realize how connected we are and how different policing techniques and violence against protesters are also exported due to globalization. One of the things that stuck with me was when I saw photos of protests around Turkey, and they had canisters of tear gas made by a company by the coast of Brazil.

And I thought, "Oh, yeah, so we're exporting these kinds of goods, like tear gas canisters to silence people in other countries?" We saw that multiple international companies were trading what they call "less lethal" weapons against protesters, and we thought, "Oh, maybe we should research more and think about how we can talk about this from the protest side, from the grassroots, from the underground."

Xuedi: We're coming from the understanding that, in our communities, activists and grassroots movements often don't have the kind of budgets to invest in tech development like governments or corporations. So how can we leverage existing tech in our favor, in people's favor? We're trying to think about tech that can be available in different types of countries. The tech available here is not going to be the same as the tech available in Asia, etc.

Pedro: It's funny, because when we talk about disruptive technologies, a lot of the time people talk about how this new startup built this new app and it's going to make millions. In our case, the real disruption or the real disobedience is to talk about protests. But one of the things that we wanted to use was this idea of appropriating existing technology in a disruptive way. So, we're trying to subvert some of the tech that's being used against the protesters and thinking about how we can communicate in a different way if they're blocking all these channels and networks.

The Dazzle Club

Emily Roderick (she/her/hers) and Georgina Rowlands (she/her/hers)

London, United Kingdom

https://www.instagram.com/thedazzleclub/

The Dazzle Club is a London-based collective of four artists who run a monthly walking club to explore the politics of surveillance in public space. Here we talk to two members, practicing artists Emily Roderick and Georgina Rowlands. Based on Computer Vison Dazzle, or CV Dazzle, a technique originally developed by artist and researcher Adam Harvey in 2010, they use bold, colorful geometric makeup to camouflage their faces against facial recognition technology. They then walk around parts of London in groups to draw attention to the pervasiveness of technologies capturing personal data without consent and also to the perniciousness of racial bias in facial recognition reference databases.

How did *The Dazzle Club* start? What made you interested in surveillance issues?

Georgina: It was a moment in August 2019. The project started in Kings Cross [central London] with the forced admission that facial recognition was being used in Granary Square. We went to Central Saint Martins University of the Arts London [located in Granary Square] and we'd studied there for four years when that letter by [Mayor of London] Sadiq Khan came out where he discussed facial recognition cameras, which had operated for an unknown amount of time. It's just the fact that it wasn't disclosed to us. It's a consent issue. If we're going to be recorded by these technologies, we want to be able to consent to them. In our project we wanted to raise awareness of the issue and expose these technologies in some way.

If we're going to be recorded by these technologies, we want to be able to consent to them. In our project we wanted to raise awareness of the issue and expose these technologies in some way.

Emily: It's about exposing changes to what we would naturally assume is a public space, when actually it's privately owned. We all have a deep connection to the area. It's the way these privately owned public spaces can be created. A lot of the time we may not know whether they're privately owned or not, and there's ambiguity around those spaces. I feel like trying to work out whether you feel welcome there—if this is a space for you. And maybe to specific people it's not a space for them. What does that mean to that space? How does that space change? So, yeah Granary Square in Kings Cross is a very bizarre place, and also very interesting to work in.

The Dazzle Club's face painting is based on a technique called CV Dazzle. Can you explain what this is?

Georgina: The original technique is developed from First and Second World War Dazzle ships. It's very geometric. A lot of the original Adam Harvey designs on the CV (Computer Vision) Dazzle website were black and white, with a few hints of color. We use more color. But color isn't necessarily important, it's more to do with strong contrasts or highlighting shadows.

Emily: Reverse contouring is a good way of explaining what it is. I don't wear makeup, so there might be a better definition, but from my understanding, contouring is where you enhance and highlight. You show more

Figure 3.5
Credit: *The Dazzle Club* / Photo: Cocoa Laney

the highlights of your face—prominent facial features like nose bridge and cheekbones. You're contouring your face into a desired face shape, a conventional beauty aesthetic. But we're very much against the shadows and highlights. We don't want to enhance things. We want to work against that. It's interesting to use makeup jargon differently.

Adam Harvey has made a very comprehensive and useful guide to CV Dazzle. He talks about five steps that you can work with or against. One of those is very much about recognizing prominent facial features and using face paint to break up those shapes and hide different parts of those features so they are no longer prominent. With CV Dazzle, the symmetrical face is kind of all chopped up and confused.

How have you adapted the concept in your work?

Georgina: We started by leading a walk around Kings Cross wearing this face paint and we had about ten people join in. We then had a discussion afterwards, which was really engaging. So we decided to keep on doing these walks and there have been twenty so far. Over time we've changed the format slightly, so it's not necessarily us leading the walks every month. We have other artists who we commission around different areas of the UK.

Emily: An artist called Robin Dowell used a kind of Faraday bag idea, where we wrapped up our mobile phones in tin foil and then carried them prominently in our hands while we walked around Plymouth. It's an open-source concept, run alongside the use of CV Dazzle, that we're using to explore what it means to be seen or not seen, visible and invisible in public space in those different ways.

We've also had face coverings with different transfers on them. And artists have made other things. It's been really lovely to open up the walks to different people to explore different ways of hiding or changing your visibility or recognition in public space.

Can you explain a bit more about how the face painting works?

Georgina: We don't paint up at home. We arrive and paint together at our meeting point. I think originally it was because participants wouldn't necessarily know the techniques around CV Dazzle, but there was also something about us coming together and teaching people about this technique, having that discussion and offering to paint someone else's face (which became such an alien thing because of COVID-19).

There's something really lovely in bringing these little paint palettes with us and something about being in that space as well. "Okay, we're here and we're going to do this together." That collective moment is really nice. We feel that we can kind of settle and reside in some of these spaces that we're walking in. Like we would just sit down and paint faces. We're there for around half an hour before we leave for the walk. It's a space to hold people.

This strange kind of face paint application is very much against what is considered the norms of makeup application. It's quite striking. It's vivid and there's a hypervisibility and for a long time you're very aware of that. And the walk is quite a nice way to try and settle yourself in that face paint. After about half an hour you forget that you're wearing it.

We always make the point of not taking it off whilst you're there. You take it off when you get home. And sometimes there are more conversations

Figure 3.6
Credit: *The Dazzle Club*

in the pub, if we go somewhere afterwards. It's important to be with other people when you've got this really bizarre face paint on—a kind of group identity. There's a comfort in that.

What happens on a *Dazzle Club* walk?

Georgina: We intentionally created a format of silent walking. One person in the group has designed a route. They're the leader. We meet at a meeting point. We apply the face paint together and the leader defines the rules of the walk, such as: we walk in silence, don't look at your phone, and don't be distracted during the walk. The walk lasts around an hour and goes around a specific area.

We find the silence, which is held throughout the route, brings focus. There're no distractions and the participants are in the moment in their bodies and listening to the city around them. We acknowledge things like CCTV cameras or security guards. It's about creating a silence in that moment to look around you and to see the infrastructures of surveillance.

As well as feeling really visible with the face paint we also feel invisible to face recognition technology. There's a defiance in walking in a big group wearing this face paint in silence. I think it's a feeling of collective resistance. And then at the end of the route we either have a discussion there or we go to a dry, warm area, like a pub, to talk about what we've just experienced.

After their first silent walk, participants are like, "Wow, I heard so many conversations and I noticed so many things that I never noticed before." I guess we're all used to walking through the city and looking at our phones or wearing headphones. The conversations are just really about people being surprised at the number of cameras or the experience of how visible they felt, but also how invisible they felt as well.

I've led a walk in Canary Wharf. We painted up and we began to walk around and the private security guards in Canary Wharf are really vigilant. There's so many of them, around every corner, and they question everybody. You can't even take your phone out and take a picture without them asking, "Why are you taking a picture?"

I remember them stopping us and questioning us: "What are you doing?" "Why are you doing it?" And we were just a group of people walking around with face paint on. We said we were a group of artists on a walk

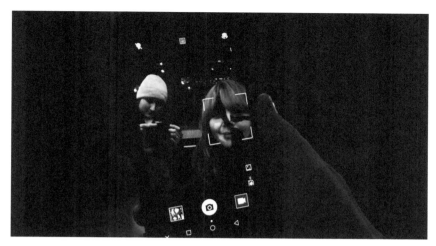

Figure 3.7
Credit: *The Dazzle Club* / Photo: Megan Jacob

and then they left us alone. But it felt really transgressive that all we were doing was wearing face paint. We weren't breaking any of the rules.

And it kind of goes back to a kind of DIY approach. We just have some color on our faces and, you know, we're not doing anything, but we are questioning our visibility. There is a resistance there. It's a visible/invisible kind of relationship.

What do you find most interesting about surveillance in public space?

Georgina: What I am most drawn to with the project is in the moment where we have participants join us on the walks. It may be the first time that they apply this face paint, and they're all very unique. We find that people's own personal self-expression comes out in the face paint. The designs are very related to their own sense of fashion or their sense of style. And when we're walking in a group, I think there's this moment where they feel very visible. They feel kind of strange, and you know, very hypervisible. But they are also aware of being invisible from the cameras' gaze. There's an interesting tension there.

Emily: The phrase that keeps coming back to us is making the invisible visible. And there's something in the act of applying that face paint. So, I think it's maybe that's what we were drawn to. Because we've worked with CV Dazzle in previous performances together. There was something really nice about applying this messy substance that works against these very specific algorithms. I think there is something quite fascinating in this DIY application that suddenly unearths a lot of questions around these very hidden technologies.

Georgina: We are interested in what this means in public space for how people can or cannot behave. We've been thinking about ideas of transgression. What it makes you feel when you're wearing these makeup designs. What do you observe and how are you observed? We're interested in the conversations people have when they put it on, how it changes or shifts how they move or interact in those spaces.

What do you observe and how are you observed? We're interested in the conversations people have when they put it on, how it changes or shifts how they move or interact in those spaces.

Emily: Before working within *The Dazzle Club*, Georgina and I were an artist duo called Yoke Collective. We've been working together since 2017, exploring different concepts and ideas around visibility, surveillance, and what it means to be a woman in front of the camera.

As well as exploring different sorts of activist techniques and tricks around the use of surveillance, or maybe working against that, and questioning these technologies and the politics around them, a lot of the time we're making performance work that responds to these research questions that come up in our practice.

Is it disguise or camouflage or trickery or is it an act of resistance, or something else?

Georgina: I like the word "camouflage," but I also like the more cosmetic relationship to makeup. Something that we talk about a little bit is the future of makeup and the future of resistance against technology and authoritarian governments and how this style of face paint and the kind of individualism and creativity it offers could integrate into a daily routine of applying makeup.

And there was actually quite a lot of coverage of the CV Dazzle technique during the Black Lives Matter protests. There were quite a few activists wearing CV Dazzle while they attended the protests. There was an article in *Vogue* by a makeup artist applying different techniques with diamantes and stickers and testing them against the iPhone camera and the different kinds of facial recognition algorithms. And it was quite interesting to see it contextualized in *Vogue*, this kind of fashion and makeup thing. I really like that.

In my mind they kind of work together like trickery. I feel tricked by the Metropolitan Police and by private security guards. I feel tricked thinking that it's public space when really it's private. I feel tricked being in Canary Wharf and a security guard comes up to you and tells you "You can't take a picture." I mean, I got the tube [London Underground] here. This is public space and they're like "No, it's private." So, I think it's countering that trickery with other trickery maybe.

What kinds of conversations are you trying to start with your creative practice?
Emily: We're trying to work out whether we should feel that we need to apply this face paint all the time every day. I think that by having these Dazzle walks, and making the space for these conversations, we're hopefully bringing awareness to these technologies that are proven to be biased. They're proven not to be useful technologies. A lot of the time they inaccurately flag up the wrong people.

I think by having these Dazzle walks and making the space for these conversations, we're hopefully bringing awareness to these technologies that are proven to be biased.

You can read about gender bias and racial bias with facial recognition. That's something we're interested in responding to and fighting against. We always have people questioning us, saying that CCTV makes us safe in public space. We always challenge them by saying that these technologies are used in really unequal ways and treat people of color, and especially women of color, really unfairly and misidentify them continuously.

Georgina: We are actively trying to opt out of being recognized by facial recognition. We're trying to resist the passiveness of being a person walking around public space and being analyzed, and having our data harvested and our biometric data read.

It's about flipping that and saying, "No, I'm not going to consent to this. I'm going to wear this makeup, which makes me invisible, and I'm going to continue walking through here and feeling the right to be in this public space." In this way, collectively walking feels like active resistance even though it's debatable how effective CV Dazzle face paint is.

In this way, collectively walking feels like active resistance even though it's debatable how effective CV Dazzle face paint is.

We know that we can test it against Instagram face filters or iPhone facial recognition and see how effective it is there, but nobody has actually been able to test CV Dazzle against Metropolitan Police facial recognition systems. We don't know how successful it is at hiding us.

Emily: But I think we're less precious about whether the CV Dazzle works now. We're more aware of the conversation and visibility that it brings to these conversations. I think, for a lot of the time, we recognize our privilege within the use of CV Dazzle. If it doesn't work, that's maybe not the main aim at this point, it's the fact that we are here. We are wearing this face paint in a space where we want to be and there's something about being in that public space that raises questions around those forms of control.

Going out and wearing it and telling people about what we're doing is a very public display of resistance. But in terms of effectiveness, we're not quite sure. It's the symbolism of us doing it that we find important.

Georgina: Even though people wore face coverings during the time of COVID-19 regulations, we've been reading about how facial recognition algorithms can recognize you from just your eyes. We know how advanced the technologies are getting. So wearing face paint doesn't really cut it any more. But we've tried different techniques like using pieces of hair over faces and using different adaptations of CV Dazzle. It feels like a bit of an arms race to catch up with it, really.

Emily: I think questions that keep coming up in conversations with *The Dazzle Club* are: What could be a future form of surveillance? Do we need surveillance? Can surveillance be kind? How could we move forward to have some sort of structure that maybe makes us feel seen rather than watched?

You know, cameras are just capturing things that may never be watched. They're just filming for the sake of filming. Are they being used? Who knows? I think visibility—and feeling seen as a person, rather than watched—is an important thing to consider.

I am THEM

Sissel Kärneskog (they/them/theirs)

Stockholm, Sweden
https://www.instagram.com/sissel.karneskog

Sissel Kärneskog is a nonbinary humanwear artist who creates wearables for queer bodies. Their designs reflect on their personal identity and experience growing up in Sweden. They start with the range of "costumes" worn by mainstream society to perform conventional relationships and then reframe them to reflect alternative narratives and meanings. Using different manufacturing techniques and aesthetics, Sissel embeds secret codes into their designs to subvert hegemonic norms of capitalism, homophobia, transphobia, and misogyny. They dress and manipulate their own body with these adapted designs to challenge accepted ideas about who gets to inhabit public space and behave in certain ways.

How do you explore identity in your art practice?

I'm interested in the gray areas in between being trans, being nonbinary, and being fluid. I grew up in a small town in the north of Sweden, and being a kid in the '90s, we didn't really discuss topics of gender, sexuality, being a lesbian or being a gay man. I never felt like I belonged anywhere. So later on, when I got older and moved to Stockholm, it was just so wonderful when I started to find the queer community. It's been like an explosion of gender identities.

As humans we think about belonging in contexts or a community. It's important to have a place to belong, to have people you can relate to, and everything that comes with it. Even the idea of being nonbinary, we have only properly discussed it for a few years, so finally when that came along, I was like, "Oh, that's me!"

I'm very happy to be able to tell my story, and that people are actually intrigued, evoking curiosity in the topics, because being queer is very stigmatized. It's kind of like disrupting tradition, because we do exist in a binary world. It's interesting to be the one who puts a fork in and twists it around a little bit.

What roles does concealment, or secrets in clothing, play in your designs?

You wear something when you go to work, you wear something when you go on a date, and you wear something when you go out with friends. And all of these are "costumes." Even though you are not playing a character, you are playing your own character. So, of course they are costumes. It all depends on the social context that you are moving within.

Something I played around with was this idea of "nearly normal." It's not really super off, but something that needs a bit of extra time to look at. Because the expectations of queerness, or the stereotype of queerness, is that it's very bombastic and extreme. I like to look at the hypermasculine and the hyperfeminine and see if there are some objects or garments that I can hack from them, and transfer into the other—the in-betweenness.

For me it's fun to speculate on hacking the context, like a social experiment of hacking the system. Because clothing is the first impression you get of someone. You see what they wear, you see what they look like, and then you speak to them.

For me it's fun to speculate on hacking the context, like a social experiment of hacking the system.

I see clothing as objects with a lot of secret codes, social codes, stereotypical codes, but especially codes around gender. The way you dress, the colors, the cut, even if you have specific designers you like, they all represent something. I have been playing around with these "normal" codes, so the suit became the thing that I started to work on. My gender identity is constantly fluid to express different versions of myself. I'm not defined in any way.

The rules of dress need to dissolve a bit, because they're still mostly around femininity and masculinity. They don't have to have anything to do with gender; it's a visual representation or an expression. A lot of people cling to it and it's very important to them, but it doesn't necessarily have anything to do with your gender.

Unisex, genderless, and androgynous, all these words work fine. But something that is unisex, I consider more as being a uniform, something that is still created for the binary. Words like genderless or gender free, well, I'm kind of full of gender.

Can you tell us about a specific piece you've made or adapted?

Being gender fluid myself, from time to time I want to cover my chest up. I want to present myself either more masc [masculine] or more fem [feminine]. I also have friends who are trans, most of them being transmasculine. I have had the conversation with them about dysphoria and, with the chest binder, the gender euphoria they feel. Through simply binding your body you can make garments fit the way they are supposed to.

Chest binders are very anonymous. They are often in different basic colors and very clean and minimalistic, so I wanted to play around with that. When I made my chest binder as a prototype and experiment, I wanted it to be elevated into something you can feel proud of wearing, that you don't have to conceal.

With shapewear, there are some knitted material technologies that are absolutely amazing. Traditionally, some chest binders are restricted to how long you can wear them, as you can actually put a lot of strain on your body. So, I wanted to play with materials that are light and just take them into a different place. It was a fun task to take something that is supposed to enhance female beauty and use it to enhance male beauty. There are so many ways we can use techniques created for the masses and actually help my community out.

I have worn this chest binder when I wanted to be masc presenting with strong sports tops and loose garments. At that time, I felt amazing. Sometimes my gender dysphoria is more and sometimes it's less. When it comes to the social costume that I talk about, it's a disguise, something worn to fit in, to be accepted, to pass. Because things that stand out, people may not understand and can often be deemed wrong. It's rare to be met with curiosity and "Oh that's fun, that's different."

Do you think that clothing can be a tool for resistance?

Clothing is the most intimate object you own, but you also take it for granted, because it's something that you just have and you need. It's not like jewelry, which is more of a luxury. Clothing is something that you constantly wear. Take the T-shirt, for example: it is a walking protest sign. The history of the T-shirt is absolutely amazing. It is one of the strongest tools you can use.

Figure 3.8
I am THEM no1.
Credit: Sissel Kärneskog

If you take a T-shirt and then you take a protest sign, the T-shirt becomes more personal because you're wearing it on your body, even though you are holding the sign in the same hand.

My community has been so silenced from the outside. It's just waiting to be able to burst out. I think, like every discriminated community in the world, it's kind of this frustration of expression. From the outside it can be extremely intimidating. Like it's something that comes with anger, but it's not anger; it's about being free and having the right to do so.

Figure 3.9
I am THEM no3.
Credit: Sissel Kärneskog

I have always been drawn to clothing, like an obsession, it's something to play around with and show my identity with, but also to disguise myself with.

Being queer, a lot of spaces are extremely intimidating to be in. So, you don't know, wherever you go in the world, if you're going to meet an ally or someone who is against you. It can be really intimidating to just be clear about who you are. This is about the idea of being brave and feeling confident to express yourself. That is also something that is dependent on where you are. When I grew up in a small town, I was really scared to express myself. I was queer before I knew what queer was.

Being queer, a lot of spaces are extremely intimidating to be in. So, you don't know, wherever you go in the world, if you're going to meet an ally or someone who is against you. It can be really intimidating to just be clear about who you are.

It was so fascinating to use clothing as a tool, in order to either fully express myself, and be the odd one out and weird, and then to be like, "I just want to be normal for a while now." I was using that almost like a disguise. So, for me, it always has been this tool. It was only when I was older that I realized how much of a tool it was.

4 CONNECTING

This chapter is about wearables that connect individuals and wider communities to important social and political ideas. From the turn of the last century, when women's rights campaigners took to Britain's streets to campaign for the right to vote, to more recent accounts of high-profile American basketball players wearing "I can't breathe" T-shirts to protest the murder of George Floyd, or environmental protesters all over the world covered in Extinction Rebellion time-running-out hourglass prints, wearables have helped people claim new forms of civic expression and render visible a wide range of inequities. Sociologist Diane Crane argues that while "histories of fashionable clothing" give the impression of consensus and conformity, a close look at clothing on the fringes of society reveals "social tensions that are pushing widely accepted conceptions of social roles in new directions."[1] So, while some wearables have historically helped those in power enforce social and physical restrictions, many have also served as emancipatory tools for people who have been denied space, voice, and rights.

Not all wearable connections are related to protest, but wearables are particularly powerful when mobilized as collective social action. Writing about the suffragettes of the early twentieth century, Wendy Parkins describes how covering their bodies in "an epidemic of purple, white and green forged a public identity for themselves in the public spaces of the city" and pushed their message "into the sphere of political communication."[2] Feminist scholar Lisa Tickner explains how these material actions were not just "a footnote or an illustration to the 'real' political history going on elsewhere, but an integral part of the fabric of social conflict" complete with "its own power to shape thought, focus debates and stimulate action."[3]

A more recent example is provided by Clothing The Gaps, an Aboriginal and Torres Strait Islander-run company in Australia, that makes and sells "Not a Date to Celebrate" and "Always Was, Always Will Be" printed T-shirts. These slogans reference and reframe January 26, currently officially recognized as Australia Day,[4] as Invasion Day, a collective day of mourning. While they make "Mob Only" pieces, most of Clothing The Gaps' collection is "Ally Friendly" for supporters to "wear their values on their tee and spark conversations." They argue that it is through "shared values and a vision to use fashion as a vehicle for social change" that collective change is possible.[5] Similarly, writing about Extinction Rebellion, geographers Eleanor Johnson and Håvard Haarstad argue that protesters' use of imagery and text, in physical, and material form, and also online, "amplified public space." They explain, "These activists and cultural influencers, these counterpublics, leverage their bodies in space to forge a new moment of storytelling that challenges the status quo of mainstream climate policy."[6]

This chapter focuses on wearables made and worn by people to connect to each other and to larger issues. In particular, we focus on clothing that unites people under a common idea or movement. As Shahidha Bari writes, "In clothes, we are connected to other people, and other places in complicated and unyielding ways."[7] In these interviews, we explore how "items of dress—from the ceremonial to the everyday—can themselves become sites of political struggle" to "contest or legitimate the power of the state and the meanings of citizenship."[8]

Rather than just highlighting problems—such as failing systems, vulnerable people, and disasters—designers in this section also use wearables to reshape public narratives. They make connections between ideas and communities to convey alternative, more positive stories about immigration, refugees, asylum seekers, and women's power. Studying these kinds of shared practices, as Diane Crane writes, can "indicate shifts in social relationships and tensions between different social groups that present themselves in different ways in public space."[9] Here, practices of connecting, in terms of organizing people and linking them to ideas via things, are explored as citizenship in-the-making.

We start with a reworking of a classic protest visual. Millions of people taking to the streets to make their voices heard over a key issue is a familiar image from 1960s civil rights movements to present day antiwar protests. In 2016, America was on the brink of the Trump presidency when old footage of Trump making derogatory, misogynistic comments was widely recirculated. The distinctive pink two-eared **Pussyhat**, with its mass appeal and wide-ranging inclusive events, challenged his narrative, reworking frustration and concerns about Trump's suitability for the role of president into a collective form of positive action that was highly visible on the streets and online. As **Krista Suh**, co-creator and co-founder of the *Pussyhat Project* explains, "A fun and successful part of the *Pussyhat* was because it was on the top of your head. When you gather together, it creates an aerial sea of pink." The fact that it was a handmade knitted hat was also central to its impact, as knitting and crocheting are often dismissed as soft feminized skills. "And yet," as Krista writes, "we know how powerful they are."

Another example that explores the extraordinary potential in everyday things is shared by artist and designer **Helen Storey**. *Catalytic Clothing*, a collaborative project with chemist Tony Ryan, explored the use of clothing and textiles to purify air and tackle the urgent problem of air pollution, an issue so large that it can feel imposing for an individual to try and remedy. "Whether it's climate change, pollution, or poverty," explains Helen, "there are some problems in the world that are so huge we often find it very hard to find what part we can play." Helen and Tony responded by coating familiar, ubiquitous denim jeans in nanosized catalytic particles of titanium dioxide using specially designed washing detergent. When worn collectively, these garments break down harmful pollutants in the air. "There was something about this technology that brought all humans together. You realize that your one part is . . . really important. It started a conversation about what humans are capable of." Innovatively every single jeans-wearer could help clean the air for fellow citizens.

Issues around immigration and asylum-seeking have become increasingly weaponized around the world. Climate catastrophes, wars, impacts of colonization, and pollution are just some of the many reasons people choose—or are forced to—flee their homes. However, their arrival in, experiences of, and sense of connection to new places are often imbued with hostility and fear. A unique perspective on the sociocultural importance of connecting across cultures and experiences is provided by **Dewi Cooke**, CEO of *The Social Studio*. This not-for-profit social enterprise uses clothing and sewing skills to forge connections between more established Australian communities and newly arrived immigrant and asylum seekers. *The Social Studio* plays a critical role in mediating different communities, breaking down barriers, and raising awareness of the vast potential that diverse communities of people bring to Australian life. Dewi explains. "There's so much for us to learn from new arrivals and people who have made these journeys to come here. They bring with them skills and abilities and cultural knowledge and craft-based knowledge that we can all only benefit from." *The Social Studio* does this by celebrating the vibrancy, diversity, and joy of multiculturalism.

Strategies for connecting to place are central to **Lucy Orta's** remarkable practice, which spans decades of groundbreaking design. Working together with partner Jorge, Lucy has been collaborating with community groups to tackle critical social and political issues around the world. This process incorporates inclusive methods and collaborative creative practice to empower and connect people on the margins of society, such as asylum seekers and prison residents. Writing about the *Modular Architecture* project, Lucy explains the need "to connect people and to build communities out of nowhere . . . to give people the possibility of feeling part of a larger whole." Her work is about developing "a feeling that you are part of a larger community with a set of values that are shared. It's about citizenship and civic-ness. Once you have acquired a sense of place, belonging, community, there is potential for your voice to resonate."

Through these interviews, this chapter shows how equality is often fought for, defended, and performed in "collective and coordinated movement in public space."[10] While very different in subject and practice, these connective wearable acts share elements of openness and surprise. Interviewees didn't necessarily know what would happen when they created the conditions for connection by bringing communities together. As Donna Haraway writes, not everything can "be known in advance of engaging in the always messy projects of description, narration, intervention, inhabiting, conversing, exchanging and building."[11] What these wearables show is how small ideas can take shape, grow in scale, and impact how change can happen.

Pussyhat Project

Krista Suh (she/her/hers)

Los Angeles, United States
https://kristasuh.com/the-pussyhat/

Krista Suh is a craftivist, writer, and co-creator and co-founder of the *Pussyhat Project*. *Pussyhats* being a distinctive handknitted pink hat with two pointy ears that gained global fame and created a highly visual "sea of pink" on the first Women's March on Washington in 2017. What is striking about the *Pussyhat* is its handcrafted ordinariness. Much like the creativity evident in protest signs and banners, each hat was uniquely handmade in pink wool. We were struck by the way such a small and mundane wearable could be used as a powerful tool for choreographing protest marches and symbolizing a collective positive and progressive message. Here Krista talks about how she uses traditional women's textile crafts like knitting and crochet as a tool for protest and community organizing.

How and when did you come up with the idea of the *Pussyhat*?

I felt very devastated by the results of the 2016 US presidential election. And I know, this is somewhat for posterity, but even now, it's hard to remember that in 2016 everyone was saying Hillary Clinton was going to win. I was so excited to have the first female US president. I had campaigned for her. When news of her loss came out, I was very, I mean, "devastated" really is the word; it can sound hyperbolic, but in this case, it really wasn't. I definitely did not feel alone in that. It really was felt throughout the US. Just a couple of days after the election, news of the Women's March started bubbling up. And I just knew immediately that I wanted to go.

I didn't know the people running it. Most of them were in [Washington] DC or gathering in DC. So the only thing I could do was really on my own person, on my own body. I decided that I wanted to do something visual on my body, because it's such a visual world. Humans are always so visual, but especially in this digital age, one striking image can just go around the world. I've always been struck by images, particularly the clash of patriarchy with feminism or femininity. I was trying to think what I could wear or what sign I could hold up. My mind sort of raced through a bunch of different ideas including just marching naked. It also occurred to me at that point that it would be very cold in DC in January. That is actually what gave me the idea. Plus, I had been really obsessed with knitting at the time. I could make my own hat. And I thought, wow, that felt right. That felt more meaningful than walking naked and, you know, certainly more cozy.

I felt there was a sizzle to making my own protest gear with my own hands. And you know, I call it magic, you could call it meaning, there was definitely significance to that. So I knew I was working with something there. And the next aha moment, so to speak, was when I realized that I was a beginner knitter and if I can make this hat, anyone could. I could see a sea of pink in front of me. Because what I'd learned about the knitting community since becoming addicted that summer, was that everyone is very generous. There's this great desire not only to make things but to give them away. I realized we could harness that power.

There's this great desire not only to make things but to give them away. I realized we could harness that power.

Can you tell us why the *Pussyhat* took such a distinctive shape and color? And what impact these design decisions made in a public protest context?

For me as an artist, even when I put together an outfit, I'm always thinking first and foremost about the silhouette. Do I stand out? Am I making a statement? With hats, the common silhouette is a hat with one point like a beanie on top. And maybe there's a pompom there, maybe it reaches a point there. And I really wanted to have two points, I had that image in my mind. One of my favorite yarn stores had a hat for children like that called the kitty hat. It was so striking because there are two points to that. And so even if you didn't see the color pink and you didn't see who the person was, it would just stand out, like, "oh, there are two points here." And I feel like people don't talk about that enough but that really sets the *Pussyhat* apart.

I just knew that women would be dropping everything, but also not dropping everything to get to the Women's March. They'd also be handling stuff at home. They'd be handling whoever also wanted to come with them.

Figure 4.1
Krista Suh.
Credit: Krista Suh

They would be planning, hypervigilant, working, stressed and tense. And I wanted that moment, where they get to the march, for someone to hand them a hat and for them to realize someone is taking care of them. They can be taken care of as well and to just have that amazing breakdown and sweet relief all at once. I was after that moment, creating that moment. Of course, I know, there are many stories. The beautiful thing about the *Pussyhat* is that everyone has their own story about the *Pussyhat*. And all of them are amazing.

The beautiful thing about the Pussyhat is that everyone has their own story about the Pussyhat. And all of them are amazing.

And I think what's interesting about the *Pussyhat*—and I know Jayna [Zweiman], my cofounder, is very passionate about this element of it as well—is that the *Pussyhat* was a tactile way for you to be there without being there in body. Instead of giving money to a cause to help hold the protest, you were creating something with your own hands. It's like that body particle, that magic particle that is transferred to the hat and sent off to that march.

There was also a backlash to the *Pussyhat*. Some people call it faculty lounge politics and that it was a little bit more like a philosophical situation versus on the ground. But of course, they're very connected. One of the main complaints was that not all women have pussies, and not all pussies are pink. Which was so funny to me in that, like, I didn't even know pussies were supposed to be pink actually, because mine isn't.

What role does handknitting and crocheting play in protest?
What we were trying to say as a whole march, not just the pussyhatters part of it, but the march itself, was that women needed to be respected. And we were not being respected in policy and culture. We were being disrespected. And yet we knew inherently, even though we forget sometimes, that we deserve respect. Knitting and crocheting as soft craft skills perfectly matched to this because they are often disrespected, considered lesser arts. And yet, inherently, we know how powerful they are. And we showed that

Figure 4.2

A crowd of people holding placards on the Women's March 2017.

Photo: Vlad Tchompalov on Unsplash, https://unsplash.com/photos/crowd-of-people
-holding-placards-KHxxCc8XMNE

at the march, so it was really intertwined, the form and the content there. And even if the average marcher couldn't articulate that, they knew it deep down; they felt it.

Knitting and crocheting as soft craft skills perfectly matched to this because they are often disrespected, considered lesser arts. And yet, inherently, we know how powerful they are.

Who would have thought that this old school thing my grandma might have done is freaking people out, right? I'm also an artist. I've shown in galleries, but I just prefer the term "craftivist" in relation to the *Pussyhats*. Art is more revered than craft. To call it art was almost buying into the patriarchal values of like, "Oh, now that we are successful, we're art now." No, we're craft. I see it as art, but I wanted to make the point of it being craft. I felt that was actually inherent to, ironically, the art of it. I feel on many different levels that, once it was successful, all of a sudden people wanted to associate themselves with it in a lot of different ways. But I just want to remind people, especially in the early parts of their creating, that actually the end stuff doesn't matter. It helps in terms of maybe soothing your ego but actually it's not a label you have to seek outside of yourself.

I think it's also about the importance of the body because there's so much machine stuff happening. There's certain crochet that machines literally can't create. There was a tweet after the Women's March where some Republican lawmaker was scoffing at it and asking, "Are these made in China?" And people were like, "No, these are handmade—how dare you!" And someone with a trained eye could actually see that those particular hats in the photo were crocheted. There's no machine that could do it like this.

The fact that they're handmade actually made it even more valuable. We were giving out something that shocked people. People give out pins or pens but no one was giving out an entire handmade piece of clothing. So, the fact that it was different, the fact that it was very luxurious, it actually meant something. It really felt like a gift people appreciated versus them just being like, "Oh, I'll do you a favor and wear this."

It's handmade, it's super meaningful, other people are wearing them, and you would be helping us by wearing them. It was a totally different experience to be a part of a march like that. And because each hat was connected to a person who made it, or who wore it, it created that bond. I chose the number 1.17 million as a goal. One, it's very like, "Whoa!" It just excites people. Two, it gets people to be like "Oh my god, they obviously can't do that themselves. I've got to help them!" And three, it was the number of people who fit on the National Mall. We wanted to have enough to give everyone one, should they want one.

Yarn stores are a natural gathering point, I think, for all sorts of life moments, it's such a community place. I wrote a letter to activate the yarn stores and basically explained to them that they could be a collection, drop off, or donation point for *Pussyhats*.

What in your opinion is the role of wearables in protest now and in the future?
I think the *Pussyhat* was so effective because it took people by surprise. Why? Because people don't respect clothing and women. It's just like how women's work is not appreciated and often not paid for. I'm not an economist, but I just think it's so fascinating that the economy would literally crumble if

Figure 4.3

Pussyhat Project knit pattern.

Credit: Krista Suh and Jayna Zweiman co-created and cofounded the *Pussyhat Project* / Kat Coyle designed the *Pussy Power Hat* / Aurora Lady created the original illustrations

we actually started paying women. So how magical is that, that you need us that badly? The reason why clothing feels so primal is because in this modern world, we don't value touch as much. And yet, clothing touches our bodies and moves with us all the time. We feel it, we create it, and we put it on ourselves. It creates this visual statement everywhere you go.

I think the Pussyhat was so effective because it took people by surprise. Why? Because people don't respect clothing and women.

I do think there's a significance with the *Pussyhat*, that it's not just a piece of clothing, but a hat in particular. I was thinking of the actual environment where we'd want to be wearing this. A fun and successful part of the *Pussyhat* was because it was on the top of your head. When you gather together, it creates an aerial sea of pink. You create something together with that. So, I think clothing is really powerful in that way. The hat also fits many body types. Even if you have a bigger head or a smaller head, there's a size for you.

I think it's so interesting that it was both very easy and very revolutionary. And I think that's what drew people to this project and to this item of clothing. Because it's easy to just plop this on your head. You don't have to zip up a whole bunch of things. It's one motion, it's so easy. It's also very eye-catching. And wearing it takes a certain amount of confidence. If not self-confidence, then confidence in your belief, in the cause. There're so many people who were happy to wear them who were like, "Oh, I never wear pink but here I'm going to do this." Some people who felt like they were breaking every rule they were ever taught in order to wear it. I think you needed both elements. Because I think if it was just easy, it wouldn't be meaningful to do it, and it wouldn't have really gathered steam.

I think putting out a design takes audacity. Putting out an outfit or expressing yourself takes audacity, and unfortunately, I think women's audaciousness is really, really dampened by our world. And, I really want to fix that. I wrote my book *DIY Rules for a WTF World* because I wanted people to know that, while I'm really proud of coming up with idea for the *Pussyhat*,[12] I actually don't think that's what makes me special. I think we all have great ideas all the time. We all have this capability. If anything makes me special, it's that I nurtured my great idea—most of us have not been taught to nurture our own creativity, which is something I had to teach myself. That's why I wrote *DIY Rules for a WTF World*, which is basically a how-to book about how to access your own creativity and bring it out, to nurture your great ideas.

It was both very easy and very revolutionary.

I don't know what technology is going to be like in the future, but whatever it is, people will respond and do things that play on the new normal. Any fashionista, or artist, or protester looks at how you effectively do something out of the ordinary. I'd like to think that this is such a punk thing to do. What makes something like the *Pussyhat* effective is that it's out of the ordinary, but it's not way out of the ordinary and so it was still in people's comfort zones.

Catalytic Clothing

Helen Storey (she/her/hers)

London, United Kingdom
http://www.catalytic-clothing.org

Catalytic Clothing is a collaborative project developed by artist and designer Helen Storey and chemist Tony Ryan. It utilizes the combined power of science and art to tackle air pollution by creating a laundry detergent that transforms garments into air purifiers. The project is a fascinating example of how ordinary items like clothing can be a powerful force for social and environmental good if applied on a large scale. Here Helen reflects on the potential of interdisciplinary collaborations, the urgency of the task she and Tony took on, and the challenges they faced when trying to get their technology adapted for contemporary business models.

What is *Catalytic Clothing* and how did it begin?

It was inspired by the comment of a twelve-year-old girl in a workshop during the project *Wonderland* (2008), where we were looking at the preciousness of plastic. She just looked up at us and said, "Why don't scientists just make more of what already exists?"

Tony, my collaborator from the University of Sheffield, was stunned by this comment and went off for a sandwich to think about it. And when he came back, we started looking at other things, not to solve necessarily, but to try and find alternative ways of addressing a social problem and the notion of air pollution landed.

We came across a form of technology to purify air that was being used on the pavements around Westminster and on a school wall in Camden. We looked at the limitations of that technology, which was basically putting the catalyst onto urban surfaces. We then thought, what if you put the technology on us? If you were to unfold every fiber of the clothes that we were wearing (in effect, a tennis court worth of surface area), this technology could utilize a surface that's not doing anything.

Clothes tell others something about our personality and what we like and don't like, what we believe and we don't believe in, the tribes we want to belong to, etc. But in technical terms, it's not doing anything. So, at that point we realized that "we" were probably the answer. If we could get that technology onto our existing clothing, it's not about buying anything new. That might be a very effective way to be able to deal with pollution. And a rather beautiful way as well.

If we could get that technology onto our existing clothing, it's not about buying anything new. That might be a very effective way to be able to deal with pollution. And a rather beautiful way as well.

The problem exists in most cities around the world. We did look at other delivery mechanisms, some ridiculous, such as: you're walking through the tube station barriers and tapping your Oyster payment card, could we spray the bottom half of your clothing for you? I find the best projects start in the area of being preposterous and then they come back down to something that's deliverable, rather than what is deemed to be practical and then

Figure 4.4
Helen Storey (University of the Arts London) and Tony Ryan (University of Sheffield) with an exhibit of a first prototype for an air-purifying dress.
Credit and photo: Tony Ryan and Helen Storey–*Catalytic Clothing*

trying to push it up to the inspirational. So, we often have very preposterous conversations.

I think when you start off with dreams, you end up with something that is more effective. And you end up with something that brings together the rational and the emotional. There's a technological solution, but if people don't (in this case) wear it, or use it, it's pointless. So, it's about the psychology behind why one does things and fitting it in with human behavior as we find it. Piggybacking our natures, rather than trying to change something seems to be the way to go, especially when you're coming up with something new that hasn't been thought of quite in that way before. Whether it's climate change, pollution, or poverty, there are some problems in the world that are so huge we often find it very hard to find what part we can play. And even if we find a part we can play, we wonder whether our tiny little action will make any difference whatsoever.

Whether it's climate change, pollution, or poverty, there are some problems in the world that are so huge we often find it very hard to find what part we can play.

What is the specific problem that you're seeking to address?
We wanted to take out as many pollutants as we could from the air. The catalytic converters[13] in cars don't, so we picked up where they leave off. But you need to have scale for it to have an impact. So, we developed the idea of putting it in your laundry powder, or laundry detergent.[14] This was the mechanism to put it onto the clothes you already own. So, it's for everybody who washes their clothes, a way to radicalize what you already own.

We discovered that denim was the most efficacious surface and then realized also that there are more pairs of jeans on the planet than there are people. If we could get it onto people's jeans, an item of clothing that people throw away the least, because people seem to form particular personal attachments to jeans. People wear their jeans in ways that they don't with other garments. So, jeans seemed to be the way.

And that was the beginning of realizing that the business model for this was going to be really challenging for people. We were speaking to a company who were massive in terms of the jeans market, and they were only interested if they could have it exclusively. They only wanted to purify the air if it was on their jeans. But there's no point doing this—clean air belongs to everybody—we are in trouble if we think we can, or should, brand the air.

How exactly does it work?

It needs movement to work and there're more of us moving around than there are buildings that could hold the same technology. It's quite basic, really. None of us walks around naked. We all wear something. We're just

Figure 4.5
Imagined packaging for *Catclo*, as a laundry product, as part of public conversations about the technology in launderettes in Manchester, United Kingdom.
Credit: *Catalytic Clothing* / Photo and box designs: DED Design

piggybacking off human nature as we find it. So, we thought, "Let's get something that is doing an incredible job for human health onto something that everybody has."

As you are walking, you are actually passing the purified air off the surface of your clothing to the person behind you. So, somebody else benefits a few seconds before you do. I think with COVID-19, we're living in a different world that might be more receptive to it now, but back then there was a question around how you promote a technology or product where someone else benefits before you, even if it's infinitesimal in terms of time. So that was a challenge as well. Now, with mask wearing being as much for others' safety as your own, perhaps *Catalytic Clothing* would stand a psychological chance.

We also looked at what different cultures wore. We realized that Indian women with their sarees were probably the most potent air purifiers on Earth. I can't remember the meterage exactly, but they wear a lot of cloth in one garment. The nature of it is quite transparent and light, so sunlight can still get through multiple layers. UV light being the trigger for the catalyst to work.

It was about looking at something that we are all doing anyway and will always do, rather than making it special in some way and therefore limiting who could have it. So it wasn't so much to do with fashion and design, it was more to do with what we all do.

How difficult is it to change existing practices?

We were trying to get it into a familiar and everyday system, hence the idea of a laundry product. You wash it onto your clothes, a bit like a two-in-one shampoo if you like and we're the conditioner. We did a huge amount of research on the impact of water. The water that puts this catalyst onto your clothing, what does it do further downstream? We found out that it actually helps sort sewage further downstream. But then in helping to sort it, it would potentially put another industry out of business, because it would be doing by default what their chemical puts into the sewer system.

We also found that it knocks out scent. And for a laundry product, that's pretty disastrous. So, whilst working with another big global company who were looking to put it into their laundry products, they realized it was a threat to all their existing ones. It speaks to a psychology of how we are convinced something is clean, by how it smells, but if there was nothing to smell, would that have a detrimental effect on your sense of wearing something clean?

It was a fascinating project, because on the one hand, it was vastly inspirational. But it very quickly started pushing at all the business models. We wanted to offer it to the world for free. We wanted to share it as a concept and share it as a form of technology. We actually looked into titanium dioxide, which was the naturally occurring compound that we were using, so we looked at if the whole world suddenly started using this product, would it become depleted?

We worked out that it wouldn't necessarily become depleted. We worked out that you only need a really tiny amount for it to be active and on your clothes forever. And that led to another challenge, which is that most companies aren't interested in selling you something once. They want you to come back and buy something again and again and again. So, then the question is, do we try and find a way to modify the dose, so that it wears off? So you have to go back and buy more. This, in terms of the world that we're living in now, feels disgusting.

It was such an interesting project because it made us realize it was an idea before its time. Even though it worked.

That is so fascinating. How did people respond to the project?

There was something about this technology that brought all humans together. You realize that your one part is really, really important. It started a conversation about what humans are capable of. It reminded everybody that we can be the smartest species on earth and we just need to think and behave differently. It's often the process of colliding disciplines that gets you to a place that neither discipline could have got you to on their own. And I've been doing that now for about twenty years and I never cease to be amazed by what comes out of a deliberate collision of creative opposites.

There was something about this technology that brought all humans together. You realize that your one part is really, really important.

Apart from when politics stopped us getting further, it was actually a very human experience that was unpoliticized as a project. There's nothing more fundamental than breathing. It's the thing we take most for granted and fear being threatened, whether it's through asthma, or what COVID-19 can do to our lungs. You're talking about something that is instinctively precious to every individual, and that cuts through politics and any other construct that you put around someone. It's the making of something that's truly and simultaneously universal and personal, and that's the power behind the project.

Can you talk a little more about what interdisciplinary collaboration brings to this type of work?

Well, I now can't imagine not doing it. I wouldn't do a project that didn't have that component in it. The nature of my collaborations has changed over the years, and the reason to design has changed over the years. But I actually find designing and sticking to a silo of a particular industry, or particular practices, is greatly limiting and to some degree a bit selfish.

It suggests that what you do is the only thing that's important. It often ties itself to career ladders. It often ties itself to the more egotistic side of creating things. What I find in colliding opposites is that there's a loosening up of the self.

Many artists would probably find different ways of saying this, but to actually be free of the self when you realize you have entered a space where there is no allegiance to what knowledge is, is amazing. But it's how that knowledge reveals itself. It's utterly thrilling to be in that space and it's life affirming for everybody involved. And once you've experienced it, you can't really go back to a single discipline.

I think it's really important to find the right human being first, who happens to be an absolute expert in an area of science. You form a bond and trust each other. Each of the scientists I have worked with, and Tony is not an exception, wanted to be able to communicate their world and knowledge more, and this project gave them another way of being able to speak of that world to a big audience. In our case, it was the area of fashion and clothes that we were in.

It's not a technical experiment in that sense. It uses the language of art and the humanity of art, to demystify the complexity of areas that ordinary human beings won't go near for fear of not being able to understand. And in that you come up with a completely new language, and often because it's in material form, it is literally beyond the limits of language.

And people become curious and connect to something without the fear of being stupid or not being clever enough to get it. Because you've given them an alternative way in. And because of COVID-19, it's become more everyday. Societal interest in the world of science has meant that science has found better ways to communicate with the general public. Everything from how can we possibly vote unless we understand the rudimentaries of science and how it affects our lives, right through to teaching young children.

If we can't find ways of grabbing their imagination, a lot of potential new scientists of the future might never gravitate towards it, and I'm particularly thinking of girls. So, it's a process of coming up with a new language. We often call it "making purple." If art is red and science is blue, we've come to a shade of purple that didn't exist before, as a way of being able to connect to the truth of what science can tell us.

What's next for *Catalytic Clothing*?

We recently put our toe back in the water because we realized that COVID-19 was giving us a democracy around the world where everybody is affected by the same thing at the same time. This is the same as air pollution. Look at the race to develop the vaccination and the speed at which we did that. Perhaps there was a temperature around that that said, "Look what we can do." "Look what we're capable of." And maybe we could piggyback on these times. The other thing we realized is that with COVID-19 testing, there are now mechanisms for being able to test things universally. So we could do a citywide trial much more easily to measure the levels of pollution that were cleaned up.

On the altruism front, we are now getting used to the fact that I wear a mask to protect you as much as to protect me, so there's also a sense of the public experiencing doing something for others on a mass scale. So, you could say that, because of COVID-19, this technology would stand its best chance to exist now. But the delivery mechanisms and the barriers between government departments, industry, and the need to make profit in particular ways still prevents it from happening.

There's a price to pay for thinking of ideas early or doing things first—it's often the second or the third entity that tries it who is the one that benefits. I've tried to develop a resilience to that, or normalize the fact that the things that we come up with often aren't yet of their time. I think it's changed recently, and I've started working a lot with Syrian refugees because there's something about being so close to that frontline that makes me outraged that things can't happen at the pace that they should happen. Refugees have a huge amount to teach us about all our futures.

But, ultimately, I think our failing is that we are, on the one hand, a spectacular species when it comes to imagining solutions, but that the current mechanisms and business models in place, and the relationships between industry and governments across different types of territorially-held departments, haven't evolved enough to enable what we're capable of doing, what we are able to improve for everyone—and that's where we get stuck, and that's why some great ideas just hang in the air.

Acknowledgments

The funders for this project were EPSRC and Ecover. The partners were University of the Arts London, Sheffield University, Ulster University, Kings College London, Centre for Sustainable Fashion, Protein, Helen Storey Foundation, Royal Society of Chemistry, Crystal Active, Future-proofed, DED Design.

The Social Studio

Dewi Cooke (she/her/hers)

Melbourne, Australia
https://thesocialstudio.org

Dewi Cooke is CEO of *The Social Studio*, a not-for-profit social enterprise that uses clothing and sewing as tools to train, celebrate, and showcase new migrant and refugee communities in Australia. The studio has helped hundreds of individuals reach their potential by creating pathways to exciting careers and opportunities. It plays a critical role in raising awareness of the vast array of possibilities and benefits that diverse communities of people bring to public life in Australia. Dewi is also a multimedia journalist and editor with broad interests in immigration, welfare, and community arts. Here she talks to us about the long-term legacy of *The Social Studio*, how it connects people together through the language of positivity, and why it is still as urgent and essential today as when it started.

What is *The Social Studio* and what does it do?

The Social Studio is a not-for-profit social enterprise. We teach clothing and textile production skills, and also skills across design, fashion, and the broader creative arts, to people from refugee and migrant backgrounds. Additionally we use art and creativity to provide social connections and break down some of the barriers that might exist for those communities to participate in Australian society, but also to showcase and highlight the inherent abilities of diverse creators and to celebrate their talents.

> *We use art and creativity to provide social connections and break down some of the barriers that might exist for those communities to participate in Australian society, but also to showcase and highlight the inherent abilities of diverse creators and to celebrate their talents.*

We're quite a complex organization. So that's the kind of broad, general statement. But within that we have a school, which teaches an accredited Certificate III in Apparel, Fashion, and Textiles, through the Royal Melbourne Institute of Technology.

We also have a manufacturing studio, which creates work for third-party clients, as well as our own fashion label. We have retail operations,

Figure 4.6
Credit: *The Social Studio* / Photo: Benjamin Thomson

where we stock products by Bla(c)k,[15] Indigenous, and culturally diverse creatives. And then we have this sort of fourth offer, which is our creative projects, and I guess community-based arts projects, where we're working across a range of artistic communities, looking for talent and collaborators. And sometimes not even looking for audience-based or product-based outcomes. We're just looking for, almost, a therapeutic outcome. We're using creativity. Like I said, it goes back to that original thread about art and creativity as a means for connection. So, there's a lot happening all the time at *The Social Studio*, which makes it a very fun and dynamic place to work but hard to distill.

The Social Studio has been around since 2009. Can you explain a little about how and why it started?

I can't take any credit for its creation. Dr Grace McQuilten had the vision—through her previous work with refugee communities and her work within the arts—to create an organization that was really tackling barriers to education for newly arrived refugee youth.

We worked with a small group of young people then from the South Sudanese community, and at that time in 2009, there was certainly a lot of handwringing within the Australian public about integration and these new communities starting up and not understanding the kind of context in which they sat. I think, to her credit, Grace, and the community of supporters that she worked with at the time, really saw how specifically fashion could be a way to reach those young people and create a safe space for them. And she'd tell you there are still some young men that she's in contact with, who talk about how transformative it was for them to have somewhere that was just theirs, where they were not judged, where there was someone who just believed in them.

And they had a fledgling brand as well, which these young people participated in and created, and they tried to sell. There was a sense of mastery that happens for people when their skills connect to their sense of self-confidence and well-being. It's the way we still operate and stay really true to those values.

It's a nonjudgmental space, a community space, that takes people as they come, I guess, and I think, importantly, probably meets our students where they need to be met. So, some students come with skills, some students come with having never sewn before, some come with dreams of running their own label, and being a fashion icon. And some students just want to learn how to sew for their kids. And that's all okay. As long as they have a goal, and a willingness to set a goal, then we can help them and facilitate whatever it is they want to achieve. I think that from the beginning, *The Social Studio* has always been that sort of place.

It really benefits from having a broad community of supporters from within the design and creative arts fields, who all want to share their knowledge and their experience. And, I think that is something that Grace helped to set in training, by necessity, because there wasn't a lot of resourcing in those early days; it was very much smell of an oily rag [getting by on a very small amount of money] or having to call in a lot of favors.

But that kind of goodwill has continued and now the Studio, even though we're a more established organization, we still believe in tapping our networks and all of our privileges and turning them over to our students or participants in whatever stream they come to us. This gives them the chance that they might not ordinarily get if they were in more mainstream education or community-based settings.

Why was _The Social Studio_ necessary then, and why do you think it is still necessary now?

It was really one of the first arts-based social enterprises to exist, I think, certainly in Melbourne. In this way, I guess there was a strong kind of foundational belief in the community-based value of what it did, in terms of working with refugee communities and asylum-seeking communities.

It was also about reframing the narrative around new arrivals to Australia, and about really looking at that through a strengths-based lens. There's so much for us to learn from new arrivals and people who have made these journeys to come here. They bring with them skills and abilities and cultural knowledge and craft-based knowledge that we can all only benefit from. So really, you know, trying to see the positive and seeing this as part of like a glorious development in our society and not a negative.

I don't think that ever stops being relevant.

There's so much for us to learn from new arrivals and people who have made these journeys to come here. They bring with them skills and abilities and cultural knowledge and craft-based knowledge that we can all only benefit from.

As an approach, Australia prides itself on being a multicultural country. It probably also believes it's a very welcoming one. And I think that we can be a small little bubble of best practice compared to what that can actually look like in practice.

And it really strikes me sometimes when I see who comes to the Studio. Last year we had students from ten different countries. And one of the sweetest friendships was between a twenty-two-year-old Congolese woman and a fifty-year-old woman from China. They're best friends, and they've gone on to do further study together now.

I just think that's the dream and what you hope for . . . to have cross-cultural connection, intergenerational knowledge sharing, and, you know, just genuine human connection. We're a little microcosm of what that can be, which I think is what makes it still necessary.

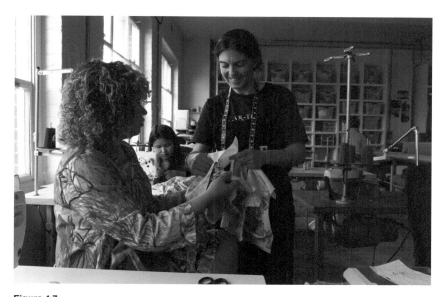

Figure 4.7
Credit: *The Social Studio* / Photo: Dewi Cooke

Very simply, why wearables? What is it about clothing or sewing that is a vehicle for social change?

I think there're a few different answers. A simple one is everybody wears clothes. You know, we all need clothes. We all understand clothes. It also goes to the idea around confidence building. Learning how to sew is a process. There is a sort of start, middle, and end. From the very basic tote bag that students begin with to, by the end of their studies with us, more complicated bodices, gowns, and pattern making. I think when you can build towards a skillset, that builds with it a sense of mastery, and that naturally builds with it a confidence and belief in yourself. It's very rewarding to, at the end of the process, have transformed a simple piece of cloth into something that has utility and function, and is also beautiful.

So, there's something that's very inherent in the process itself of clothing-making. If you step away from the practicality of what the students do, and look at it from a cultural point of view, clothing, and cloth, and how we appear across all societies, can have meaning and value. It's a way for us to communicate our cultural backgrounds, our faith backgrounds, our geographies. So, there's just a lot of rich meaning in clothing generally, right? You would appreciate that as researchers.

I think for our participants to be able to explore that is also something that's very enriching. Because, if you come from a multicultural community in Australia, maybe you don't get the chance to stamp your identity on your spaces that you interact with on a day-to-day basis as much. So this is one way, and one space, in which those students can express who they are, and perhaps where they come from. It's not always cultural clothing, but certainly their sense of style, which is very personal to each person.

Can you talk a bit more about *The Social Studio*'s *Who's Afraid of Public Space* event, because fears about difference and diversity in public space feature in a lot of public discourse.

That event on the steps of Parliament House in Victoria was an example of when fashion worn by, designed by, and made by diverse communities literally takes over a public space that is significant, symbolic. And it wasn't, like, at all political. We don't try to do political events, but it was quietly very effective because it was this celebration of diversity, but joyous and kind of unencumbered and not facilitated by those institutions. It was as though we popped up in this space, which was kind of the intention the whole time.

I thought that was a really interesting idea. I used to be a reporter, and I did a lot on, so to speak, "multicultural communities." In the early 2000s, mid-to-late 2000s, and particularly within the South Sudanese community, there were a few very tragic deaths. The young people that I spoke to at the time were talking about the struggles of just being so visible, and standing out so much physically from the crowd. It made them a target, made them more conscious of themselves walking through space and engaging with space. And then layered on top of that is just the kind of evergreen conversation around like, where do young people have a right to exist? There are playgrounds for children, and there are restaurants for adults. But, where do teenagers and young adults get to go without causing suspicion? And when you are also a young person of color, how does that work for you?

So, I think that event was a really lovely antidote, you know, to some of those concerns, because people were just able to be there and be a really positive force and show off their skills. It was a really fun day.

Figure 4.8
Credit: *The Social Studio* / Photo: Naomi Rahim

How important is this *antidote*, as you say, and the *joy* of these kinds of events and communications? Can joy be seen as a political act?

I think it still surprises me how fundraising would be a lot easier for us if we were willing to take that path and tell the trauma of a story. Audiences still kind of want to understand people's need or disadvantage, then they can figure out how they can help. And so, telling people about someone's strengths makes it harder to understand how and why they need help. And that's what we're always trying to balance. We really try to be led by how our students and participants want their stories told or represented.

Some of our students don't want to be on camera at all. And obviously we respect that. Some students love the camera, and are our poster children, and that's great for them. But what we definitely don't do, unless the students are comfortable with it, is talk about trauma, or the difficulties of life prior to coming to us. In some cases, it is relevant and possible, but we will only do that with the consent, or at the initiation of our students. I think that would be an easier narrative to present. To say, these are poor, disadvantaged, and disenfranchised people who need our help.

But instead . . . joy!

Almost a political decision itself is about choosing to say instead that these people bring light, wherever they go. Or who, through their skills and talents, are essential members of our team or have shown incredible growth. Those are the stories told at our events. It's just a reflection of how people want their story to be represented. We're not trying to shape it. It's very natural.

We want to ask a bit more about making different people's stories visible, especially for those who are, as you say, highly visible already. What other kinds of challenges or opportunities come with increased visibility?

Some students don't even identify with being referred to as refugees or having come from refugee backgrounds. They're Somali or South Sudanese or Ethiopian. The refugee label is just how they came to Australia. It isn't definitive of who they are.

And, sometimes we have to invoke that terminology because it makes it easier to talk about a group. It would be more complex to name every single country that we've ever worked with people from, because it would be a huge list. And we don't necessarily want to be prescriptive. So, I think the language we use is something that we are conscious of, and it really needs to be an ongoing conversation.

It also depends on the generation of the person that we're working with, even though we have a huge base. We have some people who are a bit older, and they might care less about language, but a young person who's come to Australia as an eight-year-old or a nine-year-old—how do they want to be? How do they want to talk about themselves and what's important to them? We are cognizant of that. Language feels like a very dynamic discourse right now. When you talk about identity and culture and communities, a lot of our students may more closely define themselves as being a person of color or according to whatever ethnic group that they originally came from, so we are sensitive to that.

And I feel like that's probably one of the things that we are working through because with that public visibility for some of our students comes those labels and we want to be able to be contemporary in terms of where they want to sit within the language.

What do you think *The Social Studio* has brought to Melbourne, to Australia, and even beyond?

Fashion is very different now with such diverse models on catwalks, in campaigns and as the face of beauty brands and stuff. It's easy to forget that just ten years ago, it was quite uncommon. And *The Social Studio* really did that. We put our student community front and center of all our campaigns and events and everything from the outset. And I don't know if we've had a hand in changing that. But I think of us as being at the vanguard of shifting fashion's lens to a more diverse, representative outlook. That is probably something that I would be happy to say that *The Social Studio* was a part of.

We've also shared our intellectual property with other organizations, such as *The Social Outfit* in Sydney. And we've had other similar organizations kind of emulate what we do, and we've not been shy about doing that because that's part of the social enterprise ecosystem: knowledge-sharing and trying to expand the model.

I like to think we were one of the first arts-based social enterprises to unite the idea of creativity and social good in a business model. That's some of our impact. We've been fortunate to come up with a few other organizations in industries at the same time working with young people from refugee backgrounds and communities. All working towards that shift of narrative. And to provide that opportunity for those young people, I think that was part of our impact on a bigger scale.

And we've had international collaborators, which has been really great. I think people come into our space and immediately sense that there's something unusual and exciting about the way we work and want to be part of it.

Are you going to keep doing what you're doing, or do you have changes in mind for the future?

I think about this a lot because I've been CEO for two and a half years now. Obviously, every leader has their own strategy, and everyone has brought a different element to this studio over its time. But I think that is a sign of its strength. There is a core understanding of what it is we do and how we do it and why we do it. And the accredited training programs are the jewel in the crown for us and what we focus on.

A bit of a personal project of mine is thinking about class. Who gets to be an artist? Who gets to be a designer? Who gets to be in an exhibition? How do we break apart the institutions that prevent or that make it harder for people to engage: "You haven't gone to the right universities," or "You haven't come from the right part of the city." If you know Melbourne, it's a very sort of scene-y place within arts and design. And we're like, let's just turn over all that opportunity to the people who come to us. It's about dismantling all those barriers to participation and getting our students and participants in there.

Somebody said to me once, in a positive way: "You guys are like the gatekeepers." And I was like, "No, that's exactly what we *don't* want be!" But then I was like, well, maybe we are. But we *open* the gate for people who don't get to go through it normally. And that's okay. We can facilitate all this experience and opportunity for people who don't get into ordinary spaces, who wouldn't get the chance. That's part of the ongoing conversation— how do we ensure that we're always turning over all those opportunities to others?

Refuge Wear and Nexus Architecture

Lucy Orta (she/her/hers)

London, United Kingdom
https://www.studio-orta.com

Lucy Orta is a renowned British visual artist committed to addressing individual body and community structures and their relation to key social and ecological challenges. Working in collaboration with her partner Jorge Orta under the banner of *Lucy + Jorge Orta*, she responds to political shifts, social inequality, and the climate emergency. A core theme of her international research concerns investigating migration and interwoven ecosystems through the medium of protective clothing apparel. Here Lucy generously shares insights from two bodies of work, *Refuge Wear* and *Nexus Architecture*, in which clothing is innovatively used as portable, modular, and autonomous survival enclosures, designed for collective well-being and community action.

Your creative work spans decades and covers a diverse range of topical subjects and outputs. How did wearables as a medium and subject matter first emerge in your practice?

While working in the fashion industry, I began making experimental clothing in response to the changing times. The first Gulf (Iraq) War broke out in the early 1990s, the consequences of which changed my trajectory. I gravitated away from fashion to reflect on clothing as a research practice. I started thinking about solutions to the humanitarian appeals for warm clothing and shelter for Iraqi and Kurdish refugees fleeing the war zones. The "clothes" I started drawing would become known as *Refuge Wear*.

The first response I made was the *Habitent*, a one-person tent with telescopic armatures that converted into a poncho. I drew on the knowledge I had of pattern cutting and the material properties of aluminum-coated fabric. I was interested in combining the different functionalities of basic human survival (by reflecting body heat from the surface membrane of the fabric), mobility (for migrant populations), and waterproofing (against adverse conditions and hardship). I saw the body as a fragile, vulnerable being that needed immediate and urgent protection. I didn't see *Refuge Wear* prototypes as clothing; they were a means of survival—something readily available, convertible, lightweight, mobile, and transformable. These concepts led me to think about the issues affecting homelessness—the idea that clothing can become a temporary shelter and a shelter becomes clothing, which might also benefit people living on the streets. Clothing could become an emergency aid—a stop-gap solution to potentially save lives.

Clothing could become an emergency aid—a stop-gap solution to potentially save lives.

Modular Architecture (1996) and *Connector Mobile Architecture* (2000) evolved out of *Refuge Wear*. These are individual bivouacs which connect via long zippers to form a communicative structure. These zips allowed for easy disconnection to avoid infringing on personal space. The modularity of these structures was an important concept, alongside the notion of flexibility. The sculptures needed to adapt to rapidly changing situations. They needed to

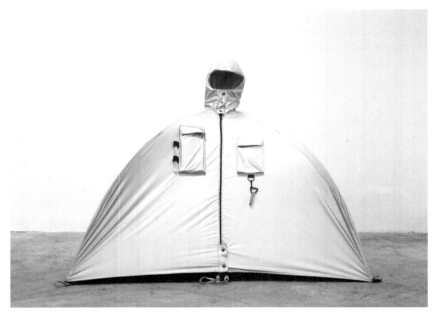

Figure 4.9
Refuge Wear–Habitent, 1992–1993.
Credit: Lucy + Jorge Orta / Photo: Pierre Leguillon

connect people and to build communities out of nowhere, to give people the possibility of feeling part of a larger whole.

They needed to connect people and to build communities out of nowhere, to give people the possibility of feeling part of a larger whole.

During the mid-'90s, I also started developing *Nexus Architecture*, exploring how clothing could tackle loneliness or indifference, or even bridge cultures by bringing people physically in contact with each other. Not just a few people, but hundreds at the same time and across continents.

After 2000, I began collaborating more closely with my partner, Jorge. Human survival and mobility remained constant subjects of our investigation. We also started working with broader societal problems such as lack of natural resources (water), environmental degradation, species loss; these became focal points for our practice.

Who are you imagining when you make your work?

While creating *Refuge Wear*, I began conversations with a group of formerly homeless people to test the survival concepts based on their experiences living on the streets. This was in conjunction with a residency that I undertook at the Salvation Army hostel in Paris in 1994. Listening and learning from them, I was able to design new functionalities according to their suggestions. But the work was never actually designed to be worn on an everyday basis; *Refuge Wear* and *Body Architecture* were experimental prototypes and they were presented in exhibitions as a public platform to engage a range of people in discussion and to draw attention to the failing social system. The attention they gained resonated with architects and designers who went on to develop functional industrial structures.

With *Nexus Architecture*, the premise of the work was to connect as many different groups of people as possible from around the world irrespective of gender, faith, color of skin, etc. A *Nexus Architecture* suit is quite simply a basic hooded worker's overall with a tube of fabric stitched on the back and front (the nexus), which connects a series of suits together via an open-ended zipper, creating an interlinked chain of wearers. This uniform item of clothing became a nonhierarchical means to negotiate relationships between people and to experiment with ways people might cooperate as a connected group. The symbolic manifestation of all the connected people gives rise to a collective body—demonstrating our fundamental human interconnectedness and that one person's actions can have huge consequences for the whole group.

Through the public performances known as *Nexus Architecture Interventions*, over the span of several years, I could metaphorically connect a range of people across continents. I also physically brought people together through staging workshops. The workshops enabled the creation of new sets of contextual suits using textiles sourced locally. In Johannesburg, we sourced local Kangas,[16] and in Hangzhou, locally woven jacquard fabrics were donated to the workshops. We chose woodblock prints in India, and we silkscreen printed the fabric with symbols and messages relevant to the local communities we collaborated with. As the work gained a reputation,

Figure 4.10
Nexus Architecture Interventions 1993–1998.
Credit: Lucy + Jorge Orta

groups who wanted to wear *Nexus Architecture* to manifest their opinions contacted me. I made a set of suits for teenagers living in a care home, specifically for their participation in the World March Against Child Labour. And *Nexus Suits* were created and worn for marches against air pollution, against climate change. The work began to take on a more political meaning in this context.

How does your practice combine possibility, practicality, and politics?

In the 1990s, I was a consultant for Premiere Vision, the textiles trade fair in Paris, so I was extremely lucky to have access to the most innovative textiles of the time. Materials became a starting point for many of the sculptures I made. I was particularly interested in new technical developments, such as the "breathable" membranes, Teflon coatings, Kevlar fibers, anti-abrasive, anti-shock, bulletproof, fire-resistant, etc. I interpreted the technical properties of the fabrics into metaphorical ideas. I designed a psychological refuge using textiles that filtered electromagnetic waves and, for *Refuge Wear Survival Sacs*, I used a thermochromic fabric that changed color to warn against freezing temperatures.

The most important aspect was the potential for the work to spark imagination, not necessarily the functionality. I wanted to prompt others to invent new solutions. *Refuge Wear* resembles anoraks, rucksacks, and sleeping bags simultaneously: the items transform, and the instructions for how to convert them are visible, printed on the fabric. Although the practical applications are inherent in the design, I hoped the work could be as open-ended as possible and function as a catalyst for new and better ideas to evolve.

I was deeply influenced by what we were living through at the time. The social and economic context of the deep global recession in the early 1990s encouraged my research practice. I was able to use clothing to express what was happening around us. Clothing had an immediacy because it was mobile and agile, flexible and modular. As I mentioned previously, I didn't see myself as a designer of clothing. I was an artist, imagining new possibilities, new futures, new spaces of habitation, of coexistence in a society that was becoming more hostile.

I think all the work I've been discussing enables a sense of place and belonging. A feeling that you are part of a larger community with a set of values that are shared.

I think all the work I've been discussing enables a sense of place and belonging. A feeling that you are part of a larger community with a set of values that are shared. It's about citizenship and civic-ness. Once you have acquired a sense of place, belonging, community, there is potential for your voice to resonate. Confidence is expressed by wearing the sculptures. For example: the teenagers who commissioned the *Nexus Architecture*, for the World March Against Child Labour. Their slogans were printed on the textiles to manifest their rights and place in the world. For this group, it was fundamental to inhabit the work, to be a visible part of a community, to take part in the march, to be at the heart of the discussion because they are the ones who are personally affected by the abuse of their fundamental rights.

What do your interventions do?
The interventions enable the work to be in dialogue with audiences. The work becomes present and active in public space and, through these public manifestations, render the invisible more visible. For example, placing *Refuge Wear* in locations around Paris, London, and New York in squats, railway stations, and subway stations was a way of drawing attention to the communities of people living on the margins and fringes of our cities.

Out of the many *Nexus Architecture* interventions, it's worth mentioning the 2nd Johannesburg Biennale (1997). This intervention was made possible through workshops with migrant Zulu women from the Usindiso shelter. Each woman made her *Nexus Suit*, choosing her fabric print as a means of self-expression. The final designs were paraded during the biennale opening and in the streets of their neighborhood.

This public intervention was very emotional because the women were so proud to show their designs, to demonstrate their strength of connectedness through the metaphor of the Nexus—the social link. During the walk, they spontaneously broke into the "Nkosi Sikelel' iAfrika", the national anthem, a significant song for the Black workers during the apartheid era. Singing that

Figure 4.11
Modular Architecture–The Unit x 10, performance at the Foundation Cartier, Paris, 1996.
Credit: Lucy + Jorge Orta / Photo: John Akehurst

out loud in public attracted other people who joined spontaneously and created a longer nexus chain, filled with Black and white passers-by not wearing *Nexus Suits*. This intervention was a potent manifestation of solidarity and connectedness, particularly after the oppression of the apartheid.

This public intervention was very emotional because the women were so proud to show their designs, to demonstrate their strength of connectedness through the metaphor of the Nexus—the social link.

The workshop also helped upskill the women with basic pattern-cutting and sewing techniques to stimulate them to become financially independent. At the end of the project, I mentioned that if the women continued to make suits to sell on the market, they wouldn't need the Nexus link. They replied, "actually, this is the most important part." So, the symbolic content of the suits became the most significant part of the garment and this was the overwhelmingly powerful outcome of the intervention.

Overall, what interests me in *Nexus Architecture* is the manifestation of the interconnectedness of human beings across continents. It's a demonstration of our solidarity with other human beings and communities. It's particularly important now that we live in such a complex period, with the rise of nationalism and the borders and fences that are being erected to divide Europe and elsewhere in the world.

5 LEAKING

In 2020 and 2021, COVID-19 restrictions in many countries around the world closed public buildings, including toilets, and severely reduced the time people could spend outside the home. For many, this might have been the first time they were spatially hindered. Yet for others, the lack of suitable toilet provisions was a familiar experience. As one journalist lamented, "For those who have periods, a disability, a medical condition or a young baby to change, public toilets aren't simply a 'nice to have.'"[1] Even at the best of times, long lines leading to women's toilets are a common sight in many places. The ability to move and dwell freely and comfortably in public space can be determined by public provisions made available to manage the discharge of bodily fluids, like urine and menses, in privacy and dignity. Inadequate facilities have prevented women and marginalized peoples from being able to fully participate in many parts of life, not just during the COVID-19 restrictions but throughout history, effectively "leashing" many to the home.[2]

Everyone urinates, and many people regularly menstruate. Yet "leaking" bodies are historically and continually viewed as problematic and shameful. Bleeding, crying, and lactating bodies have been marked as different from the "universalized" and contained male body and as such are viewed as faulty, inferior, uncontained, uncontainable, and uncontrollable.[3] Many have linked it to what anthropologist Mary Douglas has classically called "matter out of place.'"[4] As feminist scholar Robyn Longhurst explains, "Women are often understood to be in possession of insecure (leaking, seeping) bodily boundaries," and it has been "commonly thought that such bodies are not to be trusted in public spaces."[5]

Menstruation is considered a "double burden" in this respect.[6] As sociologists Natalie Moffat and Lucy Pickering argue, it "entails a lot of work" as "women must conceal both blood and the products used for this concealment whilst ensuring menstruation is not mentioned."[7] Work is required because "women's menstrual flow is regarded not only with shame and embarrassment but with the powers of contaminating."[8] The leaking body, long considered a pollutant, is forced to hide its leakage or to sanitize it in public contexts.

In this way public toilets, or lack thereof, are directly linked to ideas of citizenship. Identifying types of people who can go to the toilet safely, conveniently, and hygienically can reflect how they are valued by society. As sociologist Phillippa Wiseman observes, toilets are "one of the most fundamental spaces in which being human is acted out, spaces that are of particular concern to disabled people."[9] She writes, "Experiences of access to toilets in both public and private spheres . . . say a lot about both how our bodies are perceived, and our citizenship imagined."[10] Queer theorist Jack Halberstam writes about how these spaces limit some people's "ability to move around in the public sphere" when they become "an arena for the enforcement of gender conformity."[11] Halberstam is writing here about the "trials and tribulations" that face some people, such as butch women, when they use public toilets and parts of society make them feel "out of place."[12] Public toilets are increasingly seen as a "battleground"[13] and "a site for gender-based hostility, anxiety, fear, desire and unease."[14] An example of this is the recent influx of "Bathroom Bill" legislations in the United States that seek to prohibit transgender citizens from using public restrooms.

The evolution of changing ideas about accepted behavior, morals, and freedom of movement (as well as race, class, and gender relations) can be mapped against access to toilets outside the home. It is a concern imbued with tension and shaped by political, social, and cultural importance. In India, for example, cultural structures of class and gender fundamentally restrict some people from this basic human right. The lack of safe sanitation means many "hold it in"[15] while others are not permitted to access public toilets.[16] Urinating outdoors can expose women to danger of sexual harassment.[17] In England, levels of acceptance or disgust associated with public peeing depend "upon whose body it is that is peeing, where and when."[18] Sociologist Adam Eldridge writes about how it is more acceptable for a man to be seen urinating in public, which reflects "the continuing masculinisation of public space, particularly at night."[19] Yet the lack of toilets is felt by all bodies with full bladders, especially by the elderly or chronically ill, parents with children, and those who are pregnant or menstruating. Urban planning scholar Clara Greed studies the gendering of public space via the lack of toilets. Despite women being the most frequent users of public facilities, she writes that "the majority of providers and policy-making groups are male, and according to women toilet campaigners, 'it simply does not occur to them, it's not important to them, they don't find it a problem.'"[20]

The lack of provisions (and policing of these spaces) promotes the pervasive notion that public space is not an appropriate place for women, transgender people, nonbinary people, the elderly, or people with impairments to linger or dwell. Combined with social and cultural norms, these infrastructural privileges determine how people experience public space and the extent to which they feel welcome there. Designers in this chapter offer creative solutions to the enduring and discriminatory issue of leaking bodies. Through the wearables they have designed, they reveal and make relevant the needs of a wider range of bodies, helping people to feel more comfortable dwelling, working, or moving in public space.

Being able to relieve yourself safely and hygienically while away from the home has been the focus of **Samantha Fountain's** company for the past twenty years. The *Shewee* is a female urination device and remains one of the most well-known designs in this field. A stand-up portable urination device might not seem like a "wearable," yet it is worn on the body and enables the freedom of movement of wearers by expanding their ability to choose where and when to urinate and dwell in public. The *Shewee* has been popular for sportspeople, in military settings, and for use in hospitals, garnering further attention during the first years of the COVID-19 pandemic. As Samantha explains, "Sales really picked up during COVID-19 lockdowns. People wanted to go and see granny or mum in the garden or park and didn't want to or couldn't go to the bathroom." It is also popular with people traveling who want to avoid public restrooms. As Samantha says, "Weeing outside is just liberating."

Industrial designer **Amelia Kociolkowska** explores the challenges faced by menstruating workers in professions dominated by men. Here the challenges include storing, accessing, and disposing of sanitary items. Amelia was struck by the lack of resources for workers in many fields and started asking, "What if these professions weren't male dominated? How could the environment work differently, and better, for women?" Amelia designed *Carrie*, a washable portable pocket for storing tampons and period pads, which could be attached to the thigh and concealed under clothing. It was targeted at wearers with no available pockets or those who feared menstrual products accidentally falling out of their pockets during work. Amelia talks about how taboo menstruation still is in many professional contexts and why the lack of resources still limits many workers: "I wanted to draw attention to the fact that even in this day and age, things like periods get in the way."

Menstruation is also the focus of artist and researcher **Romina Chuls**. She is particularly drawn to challenging the stigma that remains attached to menstruation. Her art practice, *Qué Rico Menstruo*, combines embroidery and wearables with public performance. She makes artifacts using knitting and crochet techniques that represent blood and bleeding. She also runs workshops with participants to explore ideas about menstruation, reproductive health, violence against women in public space, and histories of colonialism in Latin America. Romina explains, "I think the idea of bleeding in public space is a performance. Let's take it back because it has not belonged to us women for so long." She continues to develop this work, despite receiving negative responses on social media, because she regards it as a form of activism and a subtle form of resistance: "So often we have this idea of activism and revolution that needs to be so 'masculine,' but stitching and knitting needles are [also] revolutionary tools."

Being able to manage bodily fluids in a private, safe, and timely manner impacts on many people's everyday lives. It shapes who gets to attend events, shop, travel, or work outdoors and, by extension, who remains stuck in the home. What might seem like small personal issues can become amplified by economic issues, pandemics, and other crises, such as COVID-19 restrictions. Social and cultural norms and beliefs around leaking bodies reveal which bodily needs are seen as important and which are denigrated. As Wiseman argues, "The implications of toileting are simultaneously global and local; increasingly recognised as being at the centre of what it means to have fundamental human rights."[21]

Shewee

Samantha Fountain (she/her/hers)

Yorkshire, United Kingdom
https://www.shewee.com

Samantha Fountain designed the *Shewee* in 1999 in Yorkshire, England. Its remarkable popularity since then can be attributed to the stubbornly enduring problems faced by people needing safe, clean, comfortable, and convenient ways to urinate when away from the home. The closure of public toilets during the early part of the COVID-19 pandemic exacerbated the already existing problem of a lack of public toilets for women, gender-diverse people, and disabled people. In her interview Samantha shares her thoughts on her design process and feedback she has received and responded to over the years, and reflects on how the *Shewee* continues to challenge taboos about urine, leaking bodies, and women as designers.

What is the *Shewee* and where did it come from?

Shewee is a plastic funnel that allows women to urinate whilst they're standing up, but particularly whilst they've got all their clothes on. It could just be a small pair of shorts in the summer or it could be huge winter gear. And then there's an extension pipe to add to the *Shewee* for mountaineers wearing massive down suits.

It's been around for twenty years now. Originally designed in 1999, the *Shewee* won a James Dyson Award.[22] I was at university studying product design, and there weren't that many females on the course and we had to look at areas that needed improving. Eventually I thought hang on, everyone really knows its women's public toilets. And I thought none of the guys on the course was going to touch that area.

With a *Shewee*, whether it's a nightclub or you're out with your granny for the day, you just go in and come out—so quick! You don't have to touch anything. You just walk up to a stall. Or even if you go into the cubicle, you don't have to shut the door. You just push it with your foot or whatever.

I had people contact me from all over the world after I won the award. It took another four years to start manufacturing, and I only did it because people would call me randomly. "Can we buy one?" And I'd be like "No, it was just a project at school." And then eventually I thought I'd get it off the ground.

Why was there such demand?

Much of the demand comes from women over the age of thirty who don't like squatting when they go out walking. And they love walking. I initially thought it was going to be younger people in public toilets, but younger people are able to squat because they've got the strength in their legs, so the demand flew because it was middle-aged women who just like being outdoors and always limited their liquids. As soon as they had a *Shewee*, they could just drink as much they wanted and it made them healthier. If you like walking and you just want to keep drinking, you don't want to have to keep worrying about it.

Maybe it's because people who've had kids need to go for a wee more often, because certain things are a bit weaker. So that market really flew, and it just went on word of mouth. It didn't need much advertising. It got a lot of publicity because it was helping people so much.

Figure 5.1
Credit: Samantha Fountain / *Shewee*

Weeing outside is just liberating.

And the first time you use it, it's just like a giggle. No one can see your bum. You don't have to worry about all this extra stuff. You don't have to worry about squatting down, getting up, falling over, or getting it on your shoes. We've just had this problem all the time, haven't we women? It always goes wonky. It always goes on your trousers. But when the *Shewee* came along, it's just like being a bloke. You're just like "Wow, that was easy."

Who else found the *Shewee* useful?

From there it then went into the armed forces. Women used to have to put camouflage on, like the painting for your face, but on their bums. It's dangerous, because otherwise it's literally like a big target in a different color. So, you're in green khaki, but no one's got a green bum. Or a sandy-colored bum if you're in the desert. So that was a real pain and also just humiliating. I mean, how do you ask your mates if they can help camo your bum?

The *Shewee* went into the NHS [National Health Service] for women who've been hurt in service—army, police, and fire brigade. Initially, it was for burn victims. If you've been burned badly and you're lying on a bed pan it was just easier to use the *Shewee*. You just turn it down the other way, so it just directs the flow directly into the bed pan. I've never laid down having a wee, but I imagine it gets everywhere. We also have one on the NHS prescription list. So now people can get it prescribed if they have had surgery or just urinary problems. One of my friends who cares for an older lady, she gets her to use a *Shewee*. I gave her a blue one. She said it made it fun, whereas normally helping someone to the toilet . . . you know. But she loved it.

How has the design developed over time?

We designed it into a rubber G-string so you could wear it. It stayed in place. You don't have to use your hand to hold it in place. It worked really well, and people use them if they are fighter pilots or in gliders. And then we made another rubber version for deep sea divers, who wear dry suits. A man has a pee valve, like a condom-type device that sticks onto the penis which releases urine out of the dry suit. Deep sea divers like police officers have to go down for longer than two hours. They have to take on fluid because it's really important. So, women weren't able to do it, because up until then they had to wee in nappies, which also makes you heavier.

As far as I know they haven't taken the *Shewee* up to a space station yet. Maybe they have, they just don't want to tell us because, can you imagine, the publicity would be awesome.

When we started, it was targeted at women. Because our market is thirty-plus-year-olds, we were being talked about in things like gardening magazines and the National Trust. And we found that just as many men were buying them for their wives, as women were buying for themselves. The men are probably having to wait. "Why she can't find somewhere to wee?" "She's always whining." "She needs the loo." You know, blah blah blah blah.

And so it was big at Christmas time. It was always men buying for women. Valentine's Day was also popular. But then we did quite a lot of work with people who wanted to transition. Some people use the *Shewee* as a packer. I didn't know we were helping those people, but it worked really well.

Sales really picked up during COVID-19 lockdowns. People wanted to go and see granny or mum in the garden or park and the sales went through the roof because people didn't want to, or couldn't, go to the bathroom. Also, people were traveling knowing that they couldn't use the toilet, or they were too scared to catch COVID-19. They didn't want to go into public restrooms. And you don't even have to get out of the car. You can wee into our pocket-sized toilet, the *Peebol*. That's for guys as well, so that works quite well. And if they did go to the toilet, they don't have to touch anything. And also, because you're facing the toilet, it doesn't matter if the door is not locked. Because, if someone came in the door, they wouldn't see you sitting on the toilet.

How do you want people to feel?

To be able to urinate outside freely without any concern that someone is looking at you, or that you might be attacked by an animal or a person. It really gets you back to your roots. I'm a real outdoorsy girl. I'm a paddle boarder. I'm a runner. I'm a triathlete. I just love being outdoors camping with the smoke and no makeup.

Men just take all of that for granted.

It's awesome to wee standing up. That liberated feeling whether you're up a mountain or behind a tree or because it's cold. Why should we have to think, "Oh I've got to have a warm drink before I go for a wee because I'm going to get my bum out and I might get frostbite"? It's just an extra concern that weighs us down.

I don't know if people always think it's quicker. I'm so practiced with the *Shewee* now that it's just quicker. It just saves time and women are busy, aren't they? You don't have to take your clothes off, pull them off, and put them on. It's just a nightmare. Especially if you've got wet gear on, trying to get it back on if it's been raining. So, I guess from that point of view, yeah, liberating. It's great just knowing that there's a product out there to help you. It's a shame that we need a product, but at least it's there.

How has the *Shewee* challenged conventional ideas or stereotypes?

There still aren't as many female designers or engineers as men. Studies show lots of things like car seats, seatbelts, and medicines aren't designed with women in mind. There're just not enough women in business. I'm a mum, and it's hard enough. We need to get to a comfortable stage where women and men maybe work three days a week each and share caring responsibilities. It's a shame because I can see both sides. I'm back into business now because my kids are older, but it's just impossible to do both at once without breaking yourself.

Studies show lots of things like car seats, seatbelts, and medicines aren't designed with women in mind. There're just not enough women in business.

I think that men do feel quite threatened because the negative comments I get mostly always come from them. There were a few women who were clearly nervous, and they came across rude about using the device. But it was the men who were like, "Well, why are you company director?" and "Why are you doing this?" and "Why are you doing that?" So I think there are still big barriers because we had trouble with the underwear that we came up with and the trousers that we would have liked to invent. It's just a nightmare

Figure 5.2
Credit: Samantha Fountain / *Shewee*

trying to even sell to women who are perhaps buyers because it's pushing the boundaries, and they don't feel comfortable about it.

It's a shame because there's not enough men out there thinking about these things, because they don't come up against these problems day to day. That's why product design courses tell you to look for an area you think needs improving, because unless you know an area inside out you can't even fathom what might be needed. I come up with a new idea every day for something or another.

What have people told you about their experiences of the *Shewee*?

Every time someone complained about the *Shewee*, I'd go and find some science. Some people worried about urine on their hands. Let me find out . . . surely, it's not dangerous? Sometimes it goes down your leg and you don't get a rash. But I'll find the information, then I'd use that in the marketing. It's just like sneezing, you know, it's fine.

We have to teach people about their own urine. Urine is sterile. We like to tell people that it's fine. Get it on your hands. Just give it a shake, you know. It's normal to put your pants back on without having a full-on wash daily, so it's okay.

But we've had loads of lovely comments over the years. A lot of people who use wheelchairs write and say how it's been liberating. They might have originally just sat on a cushion, but they've changed chairs so they can pull out the middle cushion, put a *Shewee* in place, attach a tube to it, and then they can go into a bag. I also get loads of people phoning, emailing, or writing letters to say thank you; it's brilliant.

I also get loads of people phoning, emailing, or writing letters to say thank you; it's brilliant.

I've heard from people from the emergency services. There are not many women in the fire brigade. They would always really sing its praises, which was lovely. Maybe because there's only ever one woman in the group. I'd say 99.9 percent can't really think of any negative. It's always been really fantastic feedback and the negative stuff would never be written. It would just be people who are nervous and a bit dismissive. Just because they don't want to use it, or we tell people to practice in the shower and they get a bit cross.

Where has the *Shewee* been and where is it headed?

There are many places that I've never been to, and yet my little babies have been all over. The *Shewee* went all the way around the world, and it's really, really, helped people. People use the *Shewee* if they want to climb Kilimanjaro, even if someone else is carrying all their gear. People have used it in disaster zones. It's the people who have gone there as support workers, and then they've given out the *Shewee*. No one has brought them in bulk yet to give to women in disaster areas. But the Red Cross take loads to give out all the time.

I'd say the word *Shewee* is well known. People know what it is versus the other things that are out there. I'd say it's a bit like Hoover. When people say I'm going to hoover, they know it's vacuuming, even though there's millions of other brands out there. So, I feel like it's the word and I don't mind if it is generic.

It might get in the *Oxford English Dictionary* eventually. I'd like to get in as a verb, because if you're standing up to wee, why not say "I'm having a Shewee"?

Carrie

Amelia Kociolkowska (she/her/hers)

London, United Kingdom
https://www.instagram.com/ameliakociolkowska/

Amelia Kociolkowska is an industrial designer based in London who believes that design can bring about important sociopolitical change. She designed *Carrie*, a garment, in the form of a detachable pocket, for storing tampons and sanitary pads, to address the inadequate provisions around menstruation that many women face on a regular basis in professions that are dominated by men, such as the police force. Her work points to larger social issues around how uniforms and personal protective equipment (PPE) in many professions are often androcentric and ignore the needs of a wider range of body types. Amelia talks to us about how ethnographic research-based design responses can offer practical and impactful solutions.

What inspires your design practice?

I was reading Caroline Criado Perez's *Invisible Women*[23] and I decided I had to do something inspired by the issues raised in the book for my final project at Central Saint Martins, University of the Arts London.

The gender data gap, and as Criado Perez also puts it, a female-shaped "absent-presence," is such an intricate issue that impacts upon so many contexts. One thing we're missing out on is that we're not necessarily being informed in the right ways to design the best products for men and women—and obviously, due to gender bias, particularly women. I really wanted to explore that and discover what is missing and realize what needs a bit more attention and care, in order to create a design intervention which would result in a better experience for women.

Your design focused specifically on women workers. What are some of the issues that struck you about women working in professions that are dominated by men?

Those who work in male-dominated professions endure the worst experiences, as various sex-specific characteristics and activities have not informed the traditional design of their work environments. For years we have witnessed women entering these industries where they have been handed a male uniform, with little to no gender-specific consideration.

These factors further fuel imposter syndrome, already an amplified issue for women in a range of careers, and of all backgrounds, but in some more often than others. I felt like there was a really good opportunity and need for bringing design thinking into these worlds and scenarios. With a social design approach, I set out to improve the experience of women in these professions. And in the process, I raised questions such as: What if these professions weren't male dominated? How could the environment work differently, and better, for women?

What if these professions weren't male dominated? How could the environment work differently, and better, for women?

I interviewed several women, ranging from workshop technicians, firefighters, police officers, and women who served in the army. I was talking to a police officer of thirty years and she said that the worst thing was when she was on her period. I thought, oh that's so standard. I also went to a police station where I undertook a ride-along and ran a workshop.

I remember I joined the meeting they had at the start of the shift, there were two men in the room, but it was mainly women on this particular team. Yet still, two men led the narrative of the meeting. When I introduced the project, they started making period jokes, like "plod on the blob." Oh my God, really? This is just what my project is about.

I found a Trade Union Congress document that reported only 29 percent of women stated that their PPE was specifically designed for women.[24] A lot of stuff they're wearing is unisex. That in itself is a really interesting discussion, because you think that the answer is always to make something unisex. I am behind this in some ways, but in contexts that are really, really crucial to keeping someone safe, it's best to recognize where people's bodies differ.

For example, some of the members of staff I was speaking with said they were trying to buy metal toe-capped boots. One of them has quite small feet. She couldn't find any that weren't bright pink and had a bit of a wedge heel. She mainly works with guys. She was like, "I want the same boots that everyone else has." I wanted to stay away from unnecessary feminization of the clothes.

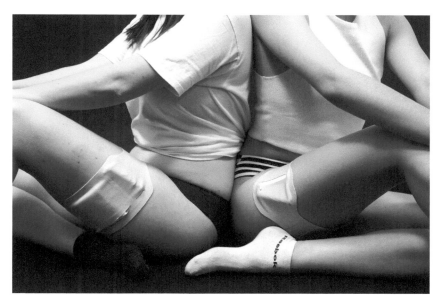

Figure 5.3
Carrie, a pocket for period products.
Credit: Amelia Kociolkowska / *Carrie*

How did your design end up focusing on menstruation and on pockets?
I was thinking about the scenarios at hand. A lot of women's clothing doesn't actually have pockets. Learning from my conversations with an ex-soldier, their experiences are the most extreme. So I thought, "What if it was something that you had on you, at all times?" "What would make it the easiest for them?" It should be kept on your body. It appeared where you needed it, when you needed it. That's where the pocket came into play.

Police officers' uniforms have several pockets—a couple on their trousers, and a couple on their vests—but they are full of lots of different things. They all use their uniforms in their own ways. The pocket, obviously, is a very practical feature of clothing. I made it separate from the uniform to make a bit more of a statement with it. A designated pocket just for your period products.

So, I came up with *Carrie*, a washable pocket for storing tampons and period pads, designed to be worn discreetly and underneath clothes. Inside the zipped pocket, there is a detachable, waterproof liner to hold used tampons and pads for when the wearers do not have the facilities to dispose of them immediately—an identified problem area.

I came up with Carrie, a washable pocket for storing tampons and period pads, designed to be worn discreetly and underneath clothes.

There are two alternative designs offering the choice to suit every preference. One is a band worn around the thigh and the other, a pocket attached and hung from the belt loop. The current prototype is made of a unique, elastic, breathable, and washable spandex for comfortable and practical wear. It would need to be quite fitted to the thigh because you wouldn't want it being a little bit too big. You don't want it being too small either, because either way it would be uncomfortable or it would fall off.

In your opinion, how visible should menstruation be?
I have quite conflicting views on this. In the conversation that initially triggered the idea, this woman was calling for discretion. She didn't want the guys in her team to know. Because when they knew, they'd start making jokes. That was, let's say, twenty years ago. But as I said, in that meeting room, they were still making jokes. Men will still make jokes about it. Not every man, not all men, but it can happen.

Sometimes I think no one needs to know that you're on your period. To me, that's not a feminist statement, necessarily. You could say that having this as a visible statement encourages the need to seek a man's approval. When in fact, it doesn't have to have anything to do with them. Each and every person might feel different about this. I'd like to explore an option that is worn on the outside as well, giving women the choice.

I've been quite fortunate enough to be in a sphere, an art institution, where talking about things like this are generally invited and encouraged. But not everyone has that sphere. Obviously, things ought to change. But I didn't feel like I wanted the women to be guinea pigs in this social experiment. There is a reluctance for women to stand out. They want to get on with their jobs and appear as equals to their male counterparts.

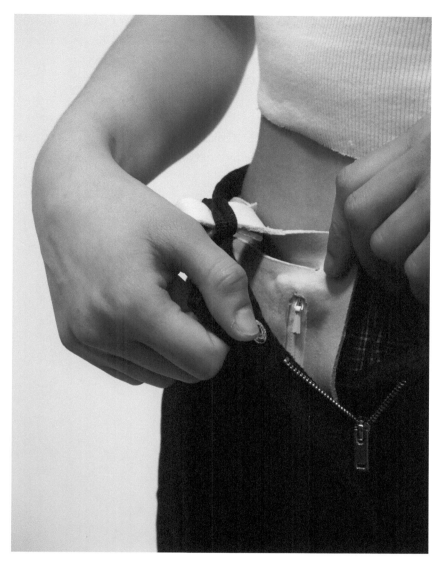

Figure 5.4

Carrie, a variation on the design.

Credit: Amelia Kociolkowska / *Carrie*

As much as this project was inspired heavily by critical thought, and I hope might one day serve as a precedent in this conversation (or at least in my practice), it is a practical design response as well. So that was where my logic came from to make it discreet.

People say it's quite a radical project, but I don't really see it as radical. That's why I get a bit disappointed when I get weird reactions to it. I wanted to open the discussion to the issues, to draw attention to the fact that, even in this day and age, things like periods get in the way.

Qué Rico Menstruo (My Delicious Period)

Romina Chuls (she/her/hers)

Lima, Peru and New York, United States
https://www.rominachuls.com

Romina Chuls is a Peruvian artist working with different textiles practices and media including, knitting, weaving, and embroidery. Her artwork has been on display in several Latin American countries and at the Textile Arts Center in New York City. She is the creator of the project and artistic movement #quéricomenstruo, which seeks to reduce the stigma around menstruation. Her knitted and embroidered textile creations are made from different-colored red threads placed on the groin area of garments and often staged in public spaces like the subway. Romina wants her art to challenge dominant perceptions about menstruation as an embarrassing and taboo subject.

Can you start by telling us about your design practice?

I am a sculpture artist that works mainly with textiles and ceramics. I work around postcolonial issues related to women and gender in Peru and also in Latin America. I get inspired by different academic research, for example, cases in Mexico about creating identity and corn harvest, also cases in the Ecuadorian Amazon on communities' displacement and how capitalism works to create gender. I'm all over the place in Latin America. I'm mainly mixing issues related to land, reproductive practices, and violence against women.

We'd like to learn more about your menstruation project *Qué Rico Menstruo*. But first, how does it translate into English?

I tried to translate it many times, but I don't know the exact words for it. It is something like "my jammy bleeding" or "my delicious period." I was looking for something related to food. Because you say "Rico" to talk about food. Peruvian culture builds itself on food. So, we use the word "Rico" to talk about many things, like you can say the beach was really "Rica" because it felt good. So, I wanted to play with this term. Some people say it means so "powerful" or "rich" but it changes completely. The term is so precise also that it doesn't translate very well to English, so I just left it in Spanish.

Figure 5.5
Pants intervened with hand embroidery, Larco Ave, Lima, Peru, 2016.
Credit: Romina Chuls / Photo: Cristias Rosas

How did it come about?

At first it was really a personal piece. I think the term is now "to soma-tize," when you're feeling psychological matters in your body. You actually feel them. And I realized that my vagina and my uterus played a great part in this. Since I was young, menstruation was something significant because it hurt a lot. And I also used to bleed a lot. It happened to me many times that I didn't manage to change on time, and I got stained. Sometimes it was not even physically uncomfortable, but it was shameful and stigmatized. And I was a teenager, and it was the worst thing that could happen to me.

This impacted me a lot. So, when I did the pants, the white jeans with red embroidery in the groin area, I was thinking well, screw it. Why do we need to go through this journey of shame and try to change and deal with it when sometimes it's not physically uncomfortable? I'm going to start making people used to seeing me with the stain, then maybe the next time I get stained they are not going to be surprised.

Figure 5.6
Underwear intervened with cross-knit looping, Union Square Subway Station, New York City, United States, 2019.
Credit: Romina Chuls / Photo: Cristias Rosas

I'm a really spiritual person, so when I'm menstruating, for me it's a sacred stage. And I'm mad that we are not seeing it like that, that society has taken that from us. I actually wore the pants day to day as a visual intervention. I wanted people to recognize that she's having this sacred moment, let's give her some love and the support she wants and have this caring environment. I deliberately use white pants, because I never used to wear white pants due to the risk of bleeding. After seeing the responses, I decided to continue with the project. It developed organically.

Why did you want to bring menstruation into public space?
I have a recurrent issue with public space because in Lima, there is no use of public space. We have a type of police that control the attitudes of people. We have strict control of public space. I grew up in a society that doesn't build community, especially in middle- and upper-class neighborhoods in Lima. Other neighborhoods are completely different. In public I've never felt comfortable. With the violence against women, it was always a matter

of keeping on your toes, being aware of everything that was happening or had happened.

I think the idea of bleeding in public space is a performance. Let's take it back, because it has not belonged to us women for so long. Maybe we can start readdressing or rethinking our ways and these violent methods.

This binary between public space and private space has been built with privatization and this practice of dispossession. I see that it has generated toxic ways of living. So how can we imagine ourselves maybe in between the tensions of the two? Or not thinking in such a binary way?

How is it different for me to bleed outside and inside?

For me it actually feels different. I feel more safe bleeding in my room. But it doesn't go with the things I need to do, because I need to take the subway anyway to go to work, to go and study. These commercials that portray menstruation like you don't feel anything and you can carry on with your day-to-day activities. No, I actually feel things and my legs get really tired. My body quits and I need to rest and that advert is not real life.

I know I should not be leaking in this public space. There is this fear that somebody will recognize that I am releasing something that I should not release in this space. Or they categorize me or allow some violent behaviors to happen that have also been related to this natural process.

I know I should not be leaking in this public space. There is this fear that somebody will recognize that I am releasing something that I should not release in this space.

When I was in New York for the first time, I started to explore the underwear with long knitting hanging from the groin area. I went through the subway and places in transit.

I understood why the presence of cross-knit looping also needed to be in this public space. I related it to the fact that many pre-Hispanic textiles got covered with Catholic motifs when colonization happened. So, we have all these techniques that got almost lost. It was also taking back this postcolonial controlled space with reencountered knitting techniques and another type of narrative. It makes sense to have this textile technique on my underwear

Figure 5.7
Performance with Peruvian artist Andrea B. Túpac Yupanqui, Punta Hermosa, Lima, Peru 2020.
Credit: Romina Chuls, performance with Peruvian artist Andrea B. Túpac Yupanqui / Photo:
Romina Chuls

in spaces like the subway; this transitional space often occupied by men. I find it beautiful to have the work there.

Why is women's reproductive health (still) such a taboo subject?

I don't know why. It sucks. And now that I'm here in the US, the Supreme Court has this threat of overturning *Roe v. Wade* [it has since been overturned]. People keep telling me because I also study abortion and talk about pregnancy interruption practices and how we can imagine it outside a neoliberalist understanding of it. So it's a more collective, more communal thinking about opportunities bigger than just the human one.

Now people are saying, "Oh your work is now important." But I come from Lima and in Peru we never legalized abortion, so it never stops. Lima is really characterized by social fascism, so the government is almost not present. But the neighborhoods and the people themselves perform a social control.

I think there is this cycle of control of reproductive rights. I take this from Silvia Federici's *Caliban and the Witch*. She talks about how capitalism was built on this desire to dispose women and people from these knowings of the earth and also from land, and control population reproduction. With Catholicism and colonialism, reproductive health was and continues to be really shameful. There is a notion that there is a shamefulness of our fluids, perceived through a loss of control with our bodies.

But being closer to spiritual traditions that relate us to more powerful forces, like the Earth and other presences, can invite other understandings of reproduction. Being afraid of losing a Western idea of human sovereignty makes us separated and hide our fluids and we just don't recognize the wholeness and the collectiveness and the other gatherings that we are participating in.

What is the link between gender issues and postcolonial land and how do you address this in your work?

I didn't realize how much I addressed colonial violence until recent years, because I relate a lot of women and feminized bodies to land and how land has been exploited for neo-extractive projects. Even if the work sometimes doesn't reflect it, my research does.

So, I grew up thinking of women's bodies as colonized territory. It addressed a colonial type of violence, colonial systems, such as militarization and the state. I saw a poster that I think is from Mujeres Creando, the collective of Maria Galindo, that says neither our bodies nor the land are territory for conquest. Also, Peru is an extremely violent country against women, and it has always had a link for me that relates to colonial issues.

I also consider future ways of thinking and new ways of creating community. Many times I'm thinking of epistemologies that live outside Western practices, but not erasing the colonial process that has created something or changed it in some way. So it's more about recognizing the tension.

Can you tell us more about the textile techniques that you incorporate into your practice?

I work mainly with one textile technique that is a pre-Hispanic cross-knit looping technique that I learned at the beginning of my professional journey as an artist. I try to work on referencing that technique in different ways. So sometimes when I use machine knitting, it's because it has a similar structure to the cross-knit looping, and I love that technique because it speaks a lot about memory itself and about a precolonial past. I say this also without a desire to speak about going back and more about imagining a new way. A new anticolonial way in the future.

Looping has this history for me that symbolizes memory and inheritance practice because you don't learn it in institutions or in the academy. You'll learn it in spaces that are not recognized as educational. Not yet. I started with textiles because my grandmother used to knit a lot. She did it beautifully by hand as a way to heal. She used to get together with women and knit and make things that weren't considered art, but of course they are.

So, it already had this gendered charge that I think passed Western thought. It holds something else. And after my grandmother passed away, I wanted to address the history of the women from my family, so textiles make sense.

Working with other women was fun, but I also love that it actually generated fear in men. Some men wrote to the group when I started exploring textiles and said, "What are you doing in there?" We were just doing textiles. So often we have this idea of activism and revolution that needs to be so "masculine." But stitching and knitting needles are revolutionary tools.

So often we have this idea of activism and revolution that needs to be so "masculine." But stitching and knitting needles are revolutionary tools.

What sort of a response did your artwork receive?

For this project, it was my first time handling social media and I had no idea it was going to be shared like that. People got really mad, and I experienced hateful dynamics and trolling. But I also created many positive responses when I open my studio. Women and friends came every Saturday, and I taught them embroidery techniques and they embroidered their clothes. A photographer friend took some photos, and we were so happy.

It was my first time handling social media and I had no idea it was going to be shared like that. People got really mad, and I experienced hateful dynamics and trolling.

Then we got another series of hateful comments. And this time they were more organized. So, the terrible thing is that these friends started to feel exposed, I'm not sure whether I didn't fully explain the risk or I didn't realize how terrible it could get. Then they began to have doubts about their interventions. I think that was the worst part of the project because I actually felt that what the project did was expose them to this collective hate and that's not the idea at all. Some people get mad and say it is really disgusting when it's an embroidery. They are lucky that it's not actually blood. Next time the smell of iron and pussy will overwhelm their senses.

But there were also a lot of positive reponses. People loved the project and I'm amazed by how long ago it was, and people are still showing it consideration and love. So, at the end it's doing more positive things and bringing this issue to the table.

How do you find the strength to go through this?

I feel it is important. That's why I cannot stop doing it. I don't know if I feel brave. Paul B. Preciado has a beautiful essay about being brave, about being himself as a trans man. He talks about how he feels he has lived with joy and not bravery. And he celebrates the lack of bravery, by the ones who lack the force to subscribe to social restrictions. I love this thought. I want a society where we aren't brave or we don't need to be. I don't feel I search for strength to do what I do. Maybe for beauty. I find comfort in acknowledging my soft moist spots. I want to be vulnerable and weak and open. I just love that.

Some people get mad and say it is really disgusting when it's an embroidery. They are lucky that it's not actually blood.

But yes, I recognize that I'm dealing with complicated issues, and I have received threats. I recognize these moments of fear because I decided to make some art. But I'm also continuing to erase the filter that was socially approved, so I know that they are going to keep coming.

6 WORKING

Ideas around citizenship and work are intimately connected. Work is a primary site of power and personal identity—shaping skills, experience, networks, and relations—as people identify themselves and others by what they do. Citizenship provides the right to work without immigration restrictions and signifies social inclusion. A job generates income, is meant to give people security, and it takes up a significant proportion of the daily lives of many adults. In an ideal system, labor comes with responsibilities, entitlements, protections, and status. Yet not all work and workers are equally recognized, remunerated, or equipped.

Analysis published by the Trade Union Congress in 2022 showed that, on average, disabled workers in England were earning 17.2 percent less than nondisabled workers (a gap increasing from 16.5 percent in the previous year).[1] As disability scholars argue, dominant narratives of full citizenship are underpinned by "ableist expectations" of full-time paid employment and this means that "the goal of inclusion of disabled persons in society through participation in work is not fully attainable."[2] Older workers similarly suffer negative workplace-based ageist attitudes and discrimination, despite laws in place to prevent this from happening.[3] Women on average remain lower paid than men and also do 75 percent of all unpaid care work globally.[4] In the United States, the gender pay gap has not changed in two decades, with women's wages still at 82 percent of the level of men's wages.[5]

Inequities like this play out not only in the processes of acquiring and retaining jobs but also in how daily working experiences are valued.

Researchers of gender and technology have long highlighted the role of those who labor behind the scenes or in less-visible sites and industries and the impact this has on the distribution of resources.[6] Susan Leigh Star and Anselm Strauss draw attention to the consequences of visible and invisible types of work.[7] They resist the idea that all work should be visible and argue that there is "good invisibility" and "bad invisibility." While the former might provide essential "backstage" support for more public front-facing practices, lesser-seen workers can also more easily be exploited, under resourced, and underpaid.[8] Writing about women workers, Judy Wajcman argues that "their absence is as telling as the presence of some other actors, and even a condition of that presence."[9] As Ruth Schwartz-Cowan reminded readers back in 1983, "Most of the people who do housework," for example, "do not get paid for it, despite the fact that it is, for many of them, a full-time job."[10]

This chapter explores work in terms of who gets equipped and resourced to do a job and who doesn't, attending to what this might reveal about perceived value of certain types of work and working bodies. What workers wear can be essential in order for them to be able to do the job, to keep safe, to project confidence or look professional, or to simply feel like they belong. Yet, many assumptions and biases map onto wearables provided for workers. For example, controversies emerged in some countries during the early stages of the COVID-19 pandemic when PPE did not fit all frontline health workers. For women (and men who are hirsuit or outside of the catered for size range), lack of appropriate protective equipment led to discomfort, injury, and infection.[11] There were reports of frontline workers having to adapt "one-size-fits-all" items or make their own. Who is and isn't provided with professional workwear, and the forms it takes, can point to wider social discrimination and practices of marginalization.

Designers in this chapter challenge inequalities by creating wearables that render visible, and possible, a wider range of professional identities. Their designs, spanning from the contexts of corporate offices to building sites, acknowledge different kinds of workers and also highlight the toxic politics of inclusion and exclusion in workspaces. These designers are members of the communities that they focus on and endeavor to help. They build on decades (if not lifetimes) of firsthand experience of many of the issues and problems facing these communities to draw attention to and develop creative ways of working around barriers. This reflects what disability activists Aimi Hamraie and Kelly Fritsch write about centering the experiences of disabled people as designers in their *Crip Technoscience Manifesto*. They highlight how disabled people have always had to "design our own tools and environments" and there are "long histories of daily adaption and tinkering."[12]

We start with **Victoria Jenkins**, the founder of clothing brand *Unhidden*, who produces garments designed by, and for, people with disabilities and chronic health conditions. Using her personal experience as a starting point, Victoria identified the lack of professional adaptivewear for disabled workers. Existing designs generally lacked flexibility in allowing for accessible fastenings and multiple access points to the body. This meant sometimes having to remove whole garments in order to change a device or administer medication. In response, Victoria designs stylish adaptable clothing that supports people in maintaining their dignity and autonomy while also looking professional in the workplace, stating, "The whole point of my designs is that the adaptations are discreet or hidden, so that if wearers are walking or rolling down the street, they're not obviously wearing something that has been adapted for them." Victoria's designs challenge stereotypes: "I think a lot of it for me came from this assumption that people with disabilities don't work, which is obviously not the case." She also advocates for more people with disabilities working in fashion industries, to help change it from the inside.

Another type of hidden working culture is revealed by **Abiola Onabulé** in her *Iyá Àlàrò* (Indigo Dyers) project. Abiola brings her Nigerian heritage—in particular the gendered histories of indigo dying and the material practice of *àdìrẹ* (pronounced "a-der-ray")—to her design practice. She combines these vibrant material practices with storytelling about the history of women textile makers and business owners in Yoruba communities. "Many fashion systems in place for hundreds and hundreds of years have been very patriarchal and very colonial. Behind the scenes, it's often very masculine in terms of who owns and manages these companies but, on the face of it, the makers are often women." Abiola's work highlights the role women have constantly played in entrepreneurial material economies. She translates these ideas into shapely, dynamic forms that exaggerate elements of the body to suggest taking up new, different physical and political positions. "Because," as she says, "so often women are described as small and not taking up too much space."

Mimosa Schmidt, founder of workwear company *SÜK* is a designer dedicated to reshaping workplace culture. Mimosa has years of personal experience of wearing ill-fitting workwear on building sites, farms, and long-haul ships—all working environments dominated by men. She explains, "Being dressed in the wrong clothes, or things that don't fit you properly, it's not just superficial. It represents something about who you are, and your identity, and it really affects your psyche. If you turn up feeling right, it does a huge amount to your confidence, and you're also read very differently." Mimosa started designing workwear for bodies ignored by conventional trade suppliers. *SÜK* is a play on "sook," a derogatory term in Australia for a person unable to cope with realities of life. She explains, "It's very universal, across all genders, but it's often dismissed as being weak or feminine or 'sooky.'" Her company is reclaiming this term by carving out space for workers ignored or harassed in unwelcoming workplaces.

The final interview in this chapter could easily sit within more than one of the themes of this book. We locate it here, partly because the interviewee appears to be constantly working, but also because the work she does shifts assumptions about the contributions of older citizens. **Debra Rapoport** is an artist of sustainable fashion pieces, necklaces, and hats. She is a member of the *Advanced Style* collective and believes in growing better with age, being creative with clothing, and honoring the planet. Debra's approach challenges conventional ideas around aging. Instead of getting smaller, more isolated, or less visible, she advocates for freedom of expression, with bold patterns and color. These ideas are reflected in her art practice. She appreciates old, often discarded things and centers recycling and sustainability in her creative practice: "I believe in curating your closet. We all own a ton of stuff, and if you owned it once, you probably still love it . . . so just bring it up front, put it together with something else." Debra runs popular workshops to teach people how to transform found objects—from toilet rolls to old cutlery—into high-end wearable apparel. Her vibrant and unique practice encourages people to look for treasure and the unexpected in each other and in their wardrobes.

The wearables in this chapter are designed for people who are overlooked, underresourced, or do not fit into conventional working environments. From a functional perspective, these designs enable workers to do their various jobs, without having to worry about wardrobe malfunctions or unsuitable clothing getting in the way. These designs draw attention to occupational as well as social and political barriers that some members of society deal with on a daily basis. As Rosemarie Garland-Thomson writes, "Misfits can also be agents of recognition who by the very act of misfitting engage in challenging and rearranging environments to accommodate their entrance to and participation in public life as equal citizens."[13] These designs confidently (and often colorfully) highlight the interests and capabilities of a broader range of people than is typically acknowledged or catered for. In doing so, they pave the way for more inclusive work cultures and expanded opportunities for work and workers.

Unhidden

Victoria Jenkins (she/her/hers)

London, United Kingdom
https://unhiddenclothing.com

Victoria Jenkins is the founder of *Unhidden*, a London-based clothing brand designed by, and for, people with disabilities and chronic health conditions. She tackles the ableism in society that manifests via clothing, especially in the context of wardrobe staples for professional white-collar work contexts. Drawing upon her personal experiences of living with an invisible disability, Victoria's adaptive designs support people with disabilities in feeling that they can express themselves, claim expert identities in the workplace, and demand to be included by the fashion industry. As she explains, so often disabled people are ignored when it comes to designing high-quality, fashionable wearables for workplaces.

What's the story behind the name *Unhidden*?

It was during a hospital stay where I met a fellow patient who changed the course of my life and switched on the light bulb. She had survived cancer, but she was left with multiple other conditions. Every time the doctors came around, she had to remove all of her clothing, usually in front of a team of doctors. Pajama tops and loungewear were her only options. She told me she wanted to dress in nicer clothes, but nothing would adapt. It was in that hospital, in front of that amazing lady, that the idea of *Unhidden* was born.

The name actually came to me at 5 o'clock in the morning, not long after I'd had the epiphany of, "I should design adaptive clothing." Because the community itself is not very well represented. It does very much feel like we're hidden, especially when it comes to invisible disabilities. It's essentially a play on words of making us unhidden and it's a common theme. As soon as I say it to someone with a disability, they know exactly where I am coming from. It's a common feeling that we are hidden and we're not really on show or given any platforms.

The whole point of my designs is that the adaptations are discreet or hidden, so that if wearers are walking or rolling down the street, they're not obviously wearing something that has been adapted for them. So they're not othered by wearing it, which is quite important. I think that is the problem with some of the adaptivewear available. The adaptation is so obvious and eye-watering you're like, "Clearly, that's only going to be worn by somebody with a disability versus somebody without one." That's why I try to keep the design discreet where I can.

What does the term "adaptivewear" mean to you?

I think it's anything that makes getting dressed easier for the wearer, that doesn't cause pain, regardless of what it is that they need. It was also about being able to access your own body because I think that's the other problem. People have catheters, tubes, and stomas. The common story I hear is having to get undressed or go to a bathroom to access things on their own body.

Figure 6.1
Credit: *Unhidden* / Model: Victoria Jenkins / Photo: Deb Burrows

I think we've come quite a long way, but not far enough. Fashion can do so many things and I think it's quite lazy to not include that; to force people to wear something that restricts you so much that not only is it uncomfortable but you can't even touch your own body in areas that you need to. It's just a bit poor, for lack of a better word.

What are you aiming to do with your designs?

I aim for dignity, comfort, and style. Dignity came from the original spark idea about how people with disabilities are already—and I use the word less and less—vulnerable because of COVID-19. I don't like that word anymore because it has horrible connotations. But for lack of a better word, I think when you are in a position where you're already really vulnerable, to then have to expose yourself in any kind of way that we don't ask of nondisabled people, it just really didn't sit well with me.

I aim for dignity, comfort, and style.

Figure 6.2
Credit: *Unhidden* / Model: Nurani

My designs aim to give back a bit of humanity to clothing. Legally we have to wear clothes, so I think there should be the option of having clothes that don't hurt you. That don't impede you. And that's where the comfort obviously comes from.

I also focus on style. This part is improving as brands are tackling it now. But conventionally, most adaptivewear is aimed at older people. It's all a bit polyester-y. It's never done from a fashion perspective where you're made to feel special or included. There's no luxury element to it. I think disabled people deserve to have a bit of fashion, a bit of luxury, and a part of the industry that they just haven't ever been given before.

Why did you choose to focus on workwear when you first launched your brand?
I mostly aim for young professionals. I just think when you want to get dressed up, there's not really that option with general adaptivewear. I think a lot of it for me came from this assumption that people with disabilities don't work, which is obviously not the case. And I thought, if they do, they're restricted because they have to wear loungewear to the office because there's not really any other choice. I think everything can be styled different ways. My designs are all in black and white because with the sustainability angle, it didn't make sense to have each design in five different colors.

I think a lot of it for me came from this assumption that people with disabilities don't work, which is obviously not the case.

I'm hoping in the future that we'll be able to put some color in. But I thought black and white are easier colors for us to routinely find because we use deadstock cloth. Deadstock is fabric left over from other companies' orders of cloth—so it doesn't go to landfill or sit rotting in a warehouse anymore.

The larger aim is true inclusion, and that comes from having access to education across a range of categories. For example, I don't think it's that common that people with disabilities can study fashion. And therefore, they don't get a design job, and they're not in the room and they are not considered. Change starts from education, human resources (HR), and hiring perspectives as much as it is actually about including them in design.

I want big brands to start to consider diverse hiring, or at least bring people with disabilities into the room with the creative team. Because I think if a load of nondisabled people start designing stuff based on what they've been told, or their research without inviting people with disabilities in, that's really problematic too. I want to hire within the community, from photographer to admin to head of HR. This is my goal.

How do you bring together accessibility, style, and sustainability?
I don't consider *Unhidden* products to be expensive. I think just everything else is cheap and we have to really focus on why that is. But I didn't want money to be a barrier to people being able to get adaptivewear. From both a sustainable and pricing outlook, I'm trialing an adaptive alteration service. It's not necessarily going to be very profitable, but it's something that I think should exist.

It might just be that people can show a five-minute video to anyone they know who can sew, or even a local dry cleaner, and have their existing clothes adapted. Eighty percent of people are not born with a disability. There're plenty of people who become disabled overnight, for example, and then what do they do with all those clothes?

So, I think rather than waste them, why don't we make those clothes work for people? People are attached to their clothes. There're so many out-fits that you don't necessarily wear all the time. Perhaps it's because they're uncomfortable or they hurt, but on a good day you'll wear them and just suck it up. But I think if we can make it so your clothes are comfortable and you can wear them more, then it's recycling and it also really helps the wearer not have to give up their entire wardrobe.

Who are your clothes designed for?
I've had so many people say, "Can nondisabled people wear it?" Of course they can. I'm just not going to directly target them. I think that's kind of offensive to my own community.

Figure 6.3
Credit: *Unhidden* / Model: Charley

The example that everyone keeps reminding me about is the crossover with maternity wear. For example, the woman's shirt bib opens. If you're breastfeeding you can then actually access your chest, again, without having to pull open the whole garment. So rather than having to get to your chest through the middle, you can also get to it via the side. That's the thing, maternity wear is technically also adaptive. They have a lot of the same properties, and I think it's so annoying that it's commonplace now to have maternity ranges and we've just stopped there. We haven't then gone, "Oh, what about for people that need all of the other differences?" I get very frustrated about it. I think people deserve to have a choice and they deserve to be represented.

There's been this willful ignorance of my community. We've existed for a long time. We're still hidden away. I think about the mental and daily struggle to put clothes on or the psychological impact of young people not seeing themselves represented. This is especially difficult if they're not born disabled and they wake up with something that they didn't have before and think: "Well, how am I going to get dressed? How am I even going to get home in the clothes I currently have?" This has long-term impact. And just seeing day by day that people aren't including you, it builds up a lot of negativity and a lot of resentment, I think, and quite rightly.

There's been this willful ignorance of my community. We've existed for a long time. We're still hidden away.

We all express ourselves through fashion. We all like to dress up and feel good and feel nice, and if you're consistently denied that, then it can be really difficult. If all you can ever really wear is loungewear, and we've all realized that since the COVID-19 pandemic, you do feel better when you feel confident and dressed up. If you want to go for a job interview but you can only turn up in clothing that fits you, which is quite often leggings for women and sweatpants for men, you don't feel professional and you don't feel involved. And you're not able to express any kind of style. I think that is something that everyone should be able to do.

How do you imagine *Unhidden* in the future?
I've said from the beginning that *Unhidden* has always been about more than just the clothes. It is very much about shining a light where it needs to be shone and giving opportunities that have been denied to the community for so long. If I can help them, then I will. And it is even better if they can work with me. I always say "with" rather than "for" because I think it's a collective arrangement that needs to happen. I've certainly tried to make a lot of noise and I think that's been good, I've managed to do that. I've certainly rattled a few cages, so fingers crossed.

Iyá Àlàro (Indigo Dyers)

Abiola Onabulé (she/her/hers)

London, United Kingdom
https://www.abiolaonabule.com

Abiola Onabulé is a womenswear designer who draws on her Nigerian cultural heritage in her practice and as a *Designer in Residence* in the Design Museum's 2020–2021 program. Under the theme of "Care," her approach entwines personal storytelling with the gendered politics of indigo dyers (*Iyá Àlàro*), who create *àdìrẹ*, a material practice that is passed down through intergenerational knowledge exchange between Yoruba women. Abiola creates unique silhouettes that amplify nonnormative body shapes. Her couture-like pieces exaggerate shoulders and hips with layers of gathered cotton and linen. These designs enable wearers to take up space and also draw attention to craft work and workers often overlooked and undervalued.

Where does your love of textiles and design come from?

I have European-Nigerian heritage. Naturally, over the years, I have collected a lot of fabrics. My family would bring them over from Nigeria. I'd play around with them and ended up incorporating them into my clothing. For my residency [called *Iyá Àlàro*] at the Design Museum in London in 2020, I continued this in the form of the indigo dyeing. I'm interested in incorporating this into my practice in a way that's not clichéd. It's not the obvious version of what it can be, because I've not grown up around that style of making in Nigeria. I've grown up with a different perspective. I think it's fun. And I've also got different things going on, different cultural forces going on. I enjoy the process of remixing and shuffling it around.

At the moment I'm telling more of a personal story in my practice. It's based on my own experiences and the things that I am exposed to. When I started the residency, I was looking at this idea of care and what care means to me and for me. It meant a lot about storytelling, especially when you're a kid. I've got lots of different influences going on in my life. And when you're a kid growing up in one country, but you've got family all over the world, stories are a very important part of that. You see those family members very rarely, but when you see them, or when you talk to them on the phone, they bring their stories with them. I have a grandfather who was Greek, who grew up in Alexandria in Egypt. And when I talked to him on the phone, he would tell tales of 1950s Egypt and his community. And that's such a key part of it. Stories have been central to my perspective.

What role do textiles play in your practice and how does this relate to the history of women's work in Nigeria?

As I was doing the residency, I was thinking about fabrics that help to formally contain narratives and I started looking close to home. On my Nigerian side, there's a whole line of women who were àdìrẹ artisans—or indigo dyers—but specifically print-based, or tie-and-dye-based indigo design. There're lots of versions of that all around the world, but this was specific and close to home in a way. I started looking further into all the storytelling that's involved in àdìrẹ. I'm especially interested in more pattern-based stuff. There's a lot of symbolism involved.

A lot of stories were centered on the idea of women's networks, because this àdìrẹ work was often very female based, specifically from Yoruba people. It was a women's craft. In the north of Nigeria, the same sort of craft is more of a men's craft. But specifically coming from my group, which is the Yoruba people, you see women having their own businesses and their families around them and supporting whole generations of people through this act of making. It was just lovely to do all the research on the storytelling around indigo dye. It felt caring in a way to be doing it for myself. You see all the things that people have done before and what generations have achieved. You can see the entrepreneurship in the community around the creativity and how much that set up an industry. Certain towns were known as places where you went to get your àdìrẹ and your indigo dyed cloth.

How do these gendered work practices relate to your personal experience?

Many fashion systems in place for hundreds and hundreds of years have been very patriarchal and very colonial. Behind the scenes, it's often very masculine in terms of who owns and manages these companies but, on the face of it, the makers are often women. And so, it always ends up feeling like a bit of a microcosm of much bigger issues.

Figure 6.4
Credit: Abiola Onabulé / Funding: The Design Museum (2020–2021 Residency) / Model:
Oré Ajala / Photo: Jessica Gianelli

Many fashion systems in place for hundreds and hundreds of years have been very patriarchal and very colonial.

I think that also ties into why I was so interested in àdìre. Because if you go back far enough, and if you look at other cultures, you can see the fallacy in the belief that women never worked. Also, it shows just how integral women were—and have always been—not just to the creativity of the culture, but also to the economy of a culture. Women have been a vital part of communities all around the world and they weren't just part of the creative act. These women in Nigeria are very entrepreneurial. They're famous in West Africa for their mercantile ways. So many women have survived on what they make and sell, with their own hands, through the years. There's a huge culture of marketplace dealings in Nigeria, and the women are tough negotiators.

On the other side of my family, there's a long history of dressmakers and of women who had set up businesses and who were able to look after their families before they got married. I was very interested in looking at all these people who were strong because of a skill that is seen as soft. A lot of the conversations we had as residents at the Design Museum were around these traditional ideas of care as a "feminine characteristic" and whether that was truly the reality. It's sometimes presented as a soft, sort of easy thing to do, but in reality, if you look at people who are in caring professions, and yes, they may often be women, it's a tough thing. It's not easy. It's very difficult. It requires a lot of action. It's not a thing that you just sit there and let happen.

How do you translate these ideas in your designs?
I make sure that everything feels nice and you can reasonably move in it, even if you want to look feminine or girly or womanly. Sometimes femininity gets tied in with restraints and constraints. In my clothes, I try to make sure that you could still be active, you could still take long strides or dance. I don't want people to walk around feeling uncomfortable. I tend to pair my clothing with quite a lot of low shoes or shoes that can be worn comfortably. That's how I always imagined it. You can run if you want to.

I've seen a lot of people dancing around in my clothes when they put them on, even when they're just doing fittings. And I think because I'm

Figure 6.5
Credit: Abiola Onabulé / Funding: The Design Museum (2020–2021 Residency) / Model: Oré Ajala / Photo: Jessica Gianelli

often using cottons which are quite lightweight or I'm using softer fabrics and because of the shapes, people want to almost test it out and see how it moves. I want people to feel taller and to feel striking, but to not be checking themselves throughout the day to see if they still look okay.

I'm trying to practice the things that I believe are possible. Making choices as you go further along to try to infuse your design with intention. I sourced cottons from Nigeria. They grow the cotton, they spin it, they weave it, and they dye it all in Nigeria. During colonial times, and then in the aftermath of English rule, they used to take parts of those processes outside of Nigeria and sell them back to Nigerians. So, I'm trying, where possible, to adjust my design process and my sourcing and research process to be in line with things that I believe in and hope for. It doesn't always work, but you just think for next time, "Okay, this is how I will adjust." It's a slow thing to build up the connections and the ability to be able to talk and work with different types of people.

A lot of your designs take up space in dynamic new ways. Can you talk more about this?

I was initially figuring out my style of pattern cutting, looking into ideas around femininity, and projected femininity, playing with that and exaggerating it. Rather than shying away from it as an aesthetic, not seeing it as good or bad, but just enjoying being like, "Yeah, this is going to be extremely big on the hips. And I'm going to make the arms look bigger. And that's okay." It's going to take up space. There's a Jeanette Winterson book called *Sexing the Cherry*, and she describes the woman in it. She's a big woman, almost like a giantess. I think that's such a lovely way to describe women. Because so often women are described as small and not taking up too much space. With my clothing, I'm changing the goal and moving away from trying to look thin, or slim, or flattering. What other things can it show? Is it expressing your joy?

Because so often women are described as small and not taking up too much space. With my clothing, I'm changing the goal and moving away from trying to look thin, or slim, or flattering. What other things can it show? Is it expressing your joy?

Figure 6.6
Credit: Abiola Onabulé / Funding: The Design Museum (2020–2021 Residency) / Model:
Oré Ajala / Photo: Jessica Gianelli

I was looking at this idea of really adding volume in areas like the shoulders, and around the chest and the hips in a way that is playing along with these traditional ideas of a feminine shape. But I wanted to exaggerate it. So, there's also a pair of trousers that are really large on the thighs and then they taper. Nowadays, maybe that sort of shaping is a lot more popular. But when I was growing up, there was no one going, "Oh, amazing, you've got thighs and a bum." No one was talking about curviness as a positive.

When I started designing, I really wanted to accentuate and celebrate that and add to it and not be scared. I didn't want someone to think, "Oh no, my hips look too big, or my arms look too chunky." I wanted to take away that worry. I'm making clothes as an exaggeration of those things. So, you didn't need to worry about whether that was supposed to be a positive or a negative.

When I think about my clothing, I'm not directly trying to make everything a political statement, but I understand the context that it's within and I understand what I'm trying to say with it. And so therefore that leads to it probably being political. And I'm okay with that, because I think it adds an interesting layer. It'd be very boring if the clothing didn't mean anything.

SÜK

Mimosa Schmidt (she/her/hers)

Melbourne, Australia

https://sukworkwear.com.au/

Mimosa Schmidt is the founder of *SÜK* [pronounced Sook], a responsive and inclusive Australian workwear company designing for a range of working bodies. With years of experience as a laborer on building sites, farms, and long-haul ships, Mimosa's designs directly address the lack of appropriate, safe, and comfortable workwear for women and marginalized workers. She identifies how, more often than not, specific clothing essential for particular working roles does not fit all bodies, and many people cannot do their jobs properly as a result. Fed up with tolerating or hacking ill-fitting menswear, Mimosa designs "tough workwear for real bodies." *SÜK* not only equips a wider range of workers but also helps them claim space and respect in work contexts that are often socially hostile places.

What does *SÜK* do and how did it come about?

I make workwear, like feminine workwear. Real, authentic, durable, comfortable, flattering, feminine workwear. The ethos behind the brand is that we don't want to leave anyone behind. I don't have any formal fashion or design training. I was a laborer and pivoted to this. I work with a pattern and garment development person and the process is very quick and extremely creative.

I spent my twenties on building sites, farms, and long-haul ships, and I just couldn't find any workwear that fitted my body. I started to mentally design other options, you know, like, obsessively. Especially when you're at work and you're hot and you're chafing, and all the dudes are looking at you funny. I kept going back to the idea of a boiler suit that fits. I would design and design and design. And then when I decided to really have a go at it, I started to make prototypes and work on patterns and think about what I was trying to do with this brand.

Being dressed in the wrong clothes, or things that don't fit you properly, it's not just superficial. It represents something about who you are, and your identity, and it really affects your psyche. If you turn up feeling right, it does a huge amount to your confidence, and you're also read very differently.

Being dressed in the wrong clothes or things that don't fit you properly, it's not just superficial. It represents something about who you are, and your identity, and it really affects your psyche.

I could never find anything that made me feel really confident. Or I couldn't find anything that reflected how confident and how capable I was that also fitted my body. And the reason why we don't have clothes like that is because we're not welcome. I never felt like I was welcome because I had to walk onto the job site looking really daggy[14] and then work three times as hard to prove I really, really, really am the real deal.

I realized that I had to address those issues in the brand as well. So, I'm always thinking about making people feel welcome and making clothes that really do work for all bodies, though I don't think that I've fully achieved that yet. There are lots of problems and issues that pop up but that truly is at the heart of what I'm doing. We're always thinking about making a size chart as accessible and inclusive as possible and having our garments translate to as many different environments and workplaces as possible.

What does the name *SÜK* mean?

I didn't realize that "sook" was only an Australian and New Zealand word. It means you're a weakling. You're emotional. You're maybe physically not intimidating and you might talk too much about your emotions. So many times on site I would hear it like almost a knee-jerk response to anything that was a too confronting, too emotionally confronting, or too intellectual. Or, like, almost too reasonable. It's this bravado thing that goes back and forth. So silly.

When I was thinking about launching the brand, all the things that make me a woman or that make me feminine were all the things that made me even better at my job. What is emotional is typically deemed to be feminine. It's very universal, across all genders, but it's often dismissed as being weak or feminine or "sooky." But it is also so vital for our community and workspaces to have this nurturing aspect and it's really sort of sacred, I think. And with *SÜK*, we say we're reclaiming the word. It really is a way of saying these things are really powerful.

Figure 6.7
Credit: *SÜK Workwear*

What is emotional is typically deemed to be feminine. It's very universal, across all genders, but it's often dismissed as being weak or feminine or "sooky."

Why is this particularly relevant for workwear?

The labor workforce landscape is still extremely masculine. In the decade that I worked as a laborer, I only worked alongside two women, which was beautiful when it happened. And if you look at the workwear landscape, it's a certain body type, and that's cis male. An athletic, broad-shouldered, cis male guy who has a certain haircut. To me that sort of sends a message that if you look different to this, or have a different body shape, maybe you're not legitimate. I would say the workwear norm is very masculine and what we're doing is extremely feminine.

When you're working, you're moving so much. You're sweating. And you really do need protection. If you're going to chafe, it is more likely that you're going to chafe when you're working, you know, because there's just simply more friction. I guess also there's the point that it could be dangerous if things are ill-fitting. You can trip over or something might get caught in machinery. It was definitely something that I noticed immediately when I started wearing boiler suits because they chafed really badly. They were drawing blood, and in places that you wouldn't imagine: around the neck, around the underarms, between the thighs, even across the belly button because the waistbands are weird sometimes. A high quantity of friction literally means more pain if you're wearing an ill-fitting garment.

There's something about women being confident, and possibly even feeling confident in their sexuality, in the context of being in a male-dominated environment that initially rubs people up the wrong way. I think there's a notion that, in expressing your femininity more boldly, you're making yourself unsafe, which I find really interesting. I would love to see that conversation turn around and say that cis men or male-dominated environments could be safer because of the expression of femininity. Subconsciously, I think they're the kind of conversations and questions that I would like to be addressed. We should be able to dress how we like and we should be able to be as feminine as we like, and still be safe.

How do you balance your designs and the rules for workplace uniforms?
We are about to enter into strictly Occupational Health and Safety (OH&S) garments and that's a whole different kettle of fish. I'm slowly approaching high-vis gear and that is quite intimidating because there are so many regulations that you have to get your head around and, obviously, it has to come in at a certain price point in order for it to be achievable.

Figure 6.8
Credit: *SÜK Workwear*

For example, if you're a woman with my body shape, when you wear those high-vis vests and it's a windy day, they just flap and it's like hanging over one tit or they're just like everywhere because they're just so big and they're not made for you. And this is something that we hear all the time. That OH&S garments aren't made for a woman; the standard is a man and a particular male body type. It's one size fits all. If you're a petite person, they just don't work for you. There are specific rules. It's something like 20 cm^2 of high-visibility color, so like orange or yellow, and then something like two meters of reflective tape or something like that. And so, you have to keep in mind that you actually need this much fabric. Then what do you do? I design everything like, "Here's the problem, how do we find a solution to this?" And I will never, ever compromise on the aesthetic. So, it's the problem and the solution.

The things at the very top of the apex are aesthetics, fit, comfort, and durability. None of those can be compromised on. If I can't find a solution, then I just put it aside and I just keep thinking on it. The other question I keep coming back to is whether this is going to be something that someone will want to wear all the time; like how much wear is really going to come out of this? If it's not a good solution, and it's not going to improve the workwear landscape or the fashion landscape, then we're just not going to do it.

What kinds of bodies do you want to clothe?

When I was dealing with all these ideas of what I was trying to do, I realized that a body shape like mine could belong to so many different types of people. And also, so many more people than just a cis woman, like myself, will want to look feminine. We know cis men that wear it.

I actually look at the design process as more of a problem-solving process. Initially, I designed these garments to solve the problems that I faced. I couldn't find workwear. In that sense I was designing for people with breasts, smaller waist, bigger hips, broad shoulders, thighs, you know, like decent thunder thighs. And then, as we launched, and we got more feedback, some people were saying, "This is great. But I would love something that fits my hips a little better," or "My thighs are super thunder thighs," you know, or "My waist is even smaller, like, I am extremely curvy." So, we have another set of problems and we go back and make a design that has a more adjustable waistband, has a wider leg, you know.

I'm trying to always share in our messaging that if you have feedback, let us know. We're always open to it. We get lots of feedback from almost every campaign that we run. In the shop it's great because people are coming in and trying things on and you can make them feel safe and have a conversation. I think the main thing is that people feel like you earnestly do want to hear that feedback.

Having never been in the fashion industry before, the feedback that I get is that it's not often an open dialogue. It's important to me for two reasons. One is that I'm very conscious about wastage. And I'm very conscious of the carbon footprint involved with fashion. And so, making things that truly are going to be used and reused is what it's all about. I'm not going to make something that isn't needed. At the moment we're not making men's workwear and that's because there are so many options for cis men. We want to make garments that really are going to be used and if that means that we have to change our design to make them more usable, that's what it's all about.

The second reason why I want to have this open dialogue is that, when it comes to the sizing, again, if it doesn't fit well, then no one's going to wear it, or they're not going to wear it for very long. Especially in the larger sizes, I think that dialogue is never really open. The feedback that I'm getting is that designers or labels will say, "Well, you're lucky even to get a size 20." I'm very driven by this idea of not leaving anyone behind and trying to make feminine bodies and all expressions feel welcome. But it's also that if we're going to do it, we really want to do it right. I have this idea that you can buy a set of *SÜK* overalls and that's all that you need to wear.

How (else) do you imagine your designs being used?

I think this has just occurred to me—what I see in my brain is an apocalyptic landscape. If you had to run out of the house and you only had one thing you could grab, it's going to be a *SÜK* overall. The reason why I have that image in my mind is that I think about how wasteful the fashion industry is. And then I think about the climate, and I think about where it's going, and I think we just can't fuck around anymore.

Figure 6.9
Credit: *SÜK Workwear*

I love useless, fun, beautiful things and I'm not saying that the kind of joy they bring into your life doesn't have value. But personally, I've always wanted to—even as a teenager—wear clothes that I can do anything in. So, for me, as someone who's very physical, that means that they have to have an element of functionality in them. And even as someone who doesn't do physical labor work anymore, those kinds of clothes are exciting for me. They definitely add an element of confidence.

We have a catchline: "*SÜK* encourages you or inspires you to be your most creative self." And I think that's sort of at the heart. There's something very true in that with clothes that really look good and are also super functional. It's like, "Oh, I could do that in this?!" I have lots of people saying, and maybe it's also a symptom of the COVID-19 lockdowns, "I got these overalls and so now I'm painting the house. I was going to call someone to do that, but now I have overalls so I'm just going to do it."

We have a catchline: "SÜK encourages you or inspires you to be your most creative self." And I think that's sort of at the heart.

We have these tradeswomen, female tradies, you know, lots of carpenters, electricians, and metal workers. I think we have a plumber. I have one customer who works in a shipyard. We also have many skateboarders and skaters, interestingly enough. We also have lots of brewers like beer brewers, gin distillers, lots of artists, cafe workers, bar workers, lots of tilers, and workers in warehouses and furniture restorers. The list kind of goes on: architects, illustrators, mural painters. I have a few cafes popping up at the moment that want to fit out their whole team and might have an all-femme crew.

I would actually say the majority of people are people who don't necessarily have a physical labor job, but they want to do physical things. And they want a pair of overalls to do it in. When I was growing up, my dad and my uncles and my grandfather, when they wanted to go and do some gardening or to service the car, they just put on their overalls. I think there are lots of customers who have been looking for that.

What change do you think *SÜK* can make in working worlds?

I've had some really terrible experiences working. I felt truly unsafe and truly belittled. I am grateful for all of it, but in many ways, it set me back. In other ways, it's made me stronger. But some of the things I went through, if I saw it happening to someone else, I would tear those people to pieces. And definitely I had a lot of anger. But where I wanted to come from with *SÜK* was like, "Don't even go there. We don't have to be angry." Anger is great, but in this I didn't want to express anger. I wanted to express joy. I wanted these garments to actually make you feel joyful and not to be a uniform for hate against toxic whatever but to be like a uniform for joy and feminine joy and feminine expressions.

I wanted these garments to actually make you feel joyful and not to be a uniform for hate against toxic whatever but to be like a uniform for joy and feminine joy and feminine expressions.

I think humor has a huge part in that: humor and happiness and keeping things light. Especially in the male-dominated, like hypermasculine space, humor is king (or queen). I've found that when I let go of anger, I feel a lot more empowered. It's more about, "Look what I can do! Look what I can do with those experiences now! Look who I can help! Look who I can inspire!"

Advanced Style

Debra Rapoport (she/her/hers)

New York City, United States
https://www.advanced.style

Debra Rapoport is an artist, designer, and member of *Advanced Style*: a collective based in New York focused on the idea of growing better with age. Photographer Ari Seth Cohen started *Advanced Style* by photographing over-sixty senior citizens in the city.[15] Together, Debra, Ari, and others celebrate individualism and freedom of expression, for people of any age, via a series of photographs, blogs, and films. Here we talk with Debra about her wide-ranging creative practice, which involves a unique relationship with found materials, and upcycled dynamic and distinctive wearable art pieces. Debra believes that older women shouldn't have to hide away and limit themselves as they age but rather embrace their personal aesthetic and live their lives however they see fit.

Can you describe your unique design approach?

Well, I call it my ABCs because that stands for assembling, building, and constructing. And I do it with color, texture, and layering. I call it "dressing up over and again" because it's a constant process and it's not about shopping and consumption and trends. It's taking what you have already and constantly making a composition on one's body, depending on who you are that day or that hour or what your activity is, what your mood is and what the weather is. So it really is a process of play. I don't take myself seriously at all. Where there is creativity, there are no rules. Where there are no rules, there is no fear.

I always tell the story about when we used to go to grandma's house, we'd go to the old sewing machine and take out the button drawer and throw the buttons on the living room floor. And my grandfather would say, "They're making a mess," and grandma would say, "Be quiet, they're being creative." Because you can't be creative without making some kind of a mess or being in a process of play or experiment.

Hopefully we can take that into our lives and take ourselves less seriously. We live in such a stressful, serious world. And it's all about success and making money. There is so much greed and corruption that we've got to get back to something basic that feeds our soul. There's too much hate, criticism, jealousy, you know. Let's get simple again.

How important is reuse and sustainability to you?

Well, Ari Seth Cohen titled me "Gifted *and* Thrifted" because people send me stuff all the time and I will not buy retail. I only go to thrift shops and now, even more than ever, they're doing amazing swap meets. I just got these pants at a swap meet. And then these socks were gifted. I think I got this sweater at a swap meet. My necklace is made up of old coat hooks and eyes.

Figure 6.10

Felt Triangular Cape with Viva Paper Hat (in the collection of Museum of Arts and Design, NYC). Credit: Debra Rapoport / Photo: Denton Taylor

I love the idea of literally sharing: like you get something for a while and you give it to a friend to wear and you see what they do with it. And then you get it back or you pass it on to someone else. Or we've done a lot of those projects where you get something, you alter it, you send it on to someone else. They'll add something more to it, or they'll embroider, or they'll add a collar or a sleeve. And that's really fun. It just keeps going and you have no idea where it's going to go and where it's going to end. But yeah, that's the beauty.

I also believe in curating your closet. We all own a ton of stuff, and if you owned it once, you probably still love it, and so just bring it up front, put it together with something else. You don't have to create one outfit and wear it the same way all the time. Mix and match and play and integrate. Don't wear one scarf, wear two or three. And if it feels like it's too much, take one off or add a fourth. Come on, it's just play. It's not brain surgery.

How does low-tech DIY practice influence your style?

What I work with, everybody can work with, it's so low tech. You don't need to be a goldsmith or woodworker to know how to work with toilet paper rolls. For many years, I worked with found metal from when cars would fall apart, and I would just walk the streets and pick it up. Now cars are plastic and they're high tech, so it's so hard to find. I found a bottlecap yesterday with a wonderful, rusted patina on it. It was like I found a diamond. Those are the things that speak to me.

I want people to wake up to their environment and see that you don't have to make a masterpiece painting. Anything is an art form. Whether it's cooking, gardening, taking care of a pet or a child, dressing up, or making stuff from found materials.

I want people to wake up to their environment and see that you don't have to make a masterpiece painting. Anything is an art form.

My favorite materials are anything that's linear and malleable, since I come from a textile background. I could just sit and twist tape and that's like a meditation. Then I'll weave with that over wire, or I'll wrap things with it. I love old used teabags, I can't throw a used teabag away because they're exquisite, especially if they get stained from the tea and they're extraordinarily strong.

Materials that I would be less comfortable working with would be something like glass. When you blow glass it's malleable, but it's not immediate enough for me to handle it. And glass is scary because it breaks. It's sharp. You have to cut it properly. It's all about the tactile. If I find something in the street, it's immediate. How do I relate to this? What is it talking to me about? How can I embrace it?

So many people say, "Oh I can't wear hats. I don't look good in them." I don't care what age, size, shape they are because I think the minute you put on a hat, it's "hattitude," right? You've got one on your head now and you can feel it. You do feel transformed and some of your personality comes out rather than hunkering down or trying to be smaller. You get larger in an expressive way.

Your designs are dynamic and attention grabbing. How important is visibility to you in terms of aging?

They say women of a certain age are invisible. Wow, what's that about? You know, when I started with *Advanced Style*, we would get letters from twenty-five-year-olds saying, "I'm already feeling invisible, it's so great to see a woman of seventy stepping out." And I said, "Can you imagine the twenty-five-year-old already worried?" It's not that we need to be seen, but we do want to be acknowledged as another human being. We just want to express ourselves and be expansive. That's all.

It's not that we need to be seen, but we do want to be acknowledged as another human being. We just want to express ourselves and be expansive.

With the availability of the internet, it's all possible. Years ago, in the '60s and '70s, I showed my work in various museums and was written up in newspapers and then when Ari Seth Cohen came along with *Advanced Style*, that gave me more visibility again in my sixties. And now with Facebook and Instagram and the continuation of *Advanced Style*, that's continued into my late seventies. And, the feedback I get on Instagram from so many people . . . they are inspired and willing to experiment, to see themselves. Then I feel okay, I have a purpose and I'm delighted to share. Any way I can inspire others—that's my calling.

When I leave the house, if people want to acknowledge and smile or take my picture, that's fine, but that's not my intention. Yes, I want to bring joy and a smile to people's faces. And if that happens because of the colors or the combination of things I'm wearing, yes, I'm totally happy to do that.

I just think we don't have to be invisible.

I just think we don't have to be invisible.

How important is the role of the body in your design practice?

I think it came from uncomfortability in my own body. Personal style is healing because it's very much about you expressing your true self and, again, it's not about fashion and trends. And that's why the pieces that I built in the late '60s were bigger than the body. They were environments. The body wasn't as important as the energy within. They were performance pieces. They were not apparel.

I told my whole back story as a younger teenager, and I did not have the perfect body. I was flat-chested (which I'm grateful for now) and I didn't feel like a very attractive teenager. So I had to reinvent myself, or reinvent how I wanted to feel in my body. That's when I started with the layering and colors and textures to distract from what a normal teenager would probably wear, like a very tight pair of shorts and a tight T-shirt or whatever. That was not my style.

Having been a young woman without the perfect body, you know, so I layered colored hats. I believe in framing the face, so that when you walk into a room, you want your face to shine. You don't necessarily want to be sexualized by having guys whistle at you for your tits and your ass. I mean we have them. And we can flaunt them. There's nothing wrong with that. But let's get past it. Let it be our energy and our exuberance that is expressed. And not flaunt the body parts, because we're more than that.

Figure 6.11

Epaulets of Recycled Materials with Head Piece (in the collection of National Gallery of Victoria, Melbourne, Australia).

Credit: Debra Rapoport / Photo: Denton Taylor

How would you explain your approach to others?

I like to think of it as the flow of life. I'm trying to get people to open their eyes and be heard more. I'm not really an activist in the political sense, but I'm an activist because I am doing and living what I believe in. That's what I want everybody else to do: to find their truth and define the way of life that they want to live in. And, ideally, it's honoring the planet. That to me is the ultimate.

How can we honor the planet?

Well, just being aware of waste and excess. Sustainability is using things over and over again. You don't throw something away when it can still be used or

Figure 6.12

Free Formed Straw Hat and Cuffs of Repurposed Materials.

Credit: Debra Rapoport / Photo: Denton Taylor

is vital. And if you don't want to use it, you pass it on. The same with food: try not to throw food out. Try to keep the scraps and turn it into stock or soup or something. And eat fresh food. Just eat real food. Eat with color, eat with texture, and enjoy every bite of it.

And appreciate health and healing. To grow older, if you don't have your health, then it's not going to be fun and playful. You've got to take care of yourself, you've got to be respectful of your body. You only have one. And now with global warming and the global climate emergency, to become vegan, or at least do Meatless Mondays, or be aware of what you're eating and how you are eating, is all part of it. Because we are part of this planet, and we only have this planet. I'm not going to Mars any time soon.

7 CONCLUSION: MAKING AND WEARING NEW CIVIC AND SOCIAL FUTURES

Wearable Utopias has explored the role of what we wear in relation to citizenship and civic concerns, illustrated by the work of designers committed to making new, more inclusive worlds for more people. We brought together the visions of twenty-six groundbreaking contemporary inventors, hackers, makers, and menders who are forging creative and critical practices that resist, subvert, and disrupt normative assumptions that shape everyday life. From anti-surveillance coats to modest swimwear, we showed how ideas in wearable form can be tools of expression, refusals to submit to restrictive ideals, and joyful acts of resistance. Here, wearables are more than simply "things that can be worn." They are world-making and -changing devices that render visible alternative futures via glimpses of new, more expansive worlds and envisioning fresh ways of inhabiting existing ones.

In this final chapter, we map some of the key ideas emerging across this collection. We build on our analysis that organised the interviews into six themes relating to different "acts of citizenship": *expanding* (wearables that push physical, social, and political boundaries); *moving* (wearables that enable participation in a wider range of sport and activities); *concealing* (wearables that defend privacy or keep secrets); *connecting* (wearables that link individuals to large scale issues); *leaking* (wearables that challenge the idea that urinating and menstruating are problematic or taboo); and *working* (wearables that address inequalities in the workplace). The designers featured in these interviews have highlighted, questioned, negotiated, and reframed issues, problems, and bodies with their designs—queering landscapes and bravely mapping new paths through and around conventional norms. Maps are social and political instruments that reveal relationships across space and time, mark significance, and inspire imaginings of travel. Ending with a mapping feels fitting, given the multiple "desire lines" we have followed in the preceding pages.

In the early 1990s, STS scholars Wiebe Bijker and John Law invited readers to consider how things "might have been otherwise."[1] They argued that technologies are never firm or fixed or determinately set in only one direction. Rather, they are designed and pressed into shape by everyday practices, decisions, and assumptions. Their heterogeneous uses, workings, and failings simply "mirror our societies."[2] This means things might have been different if alternative paths were taken or new questions asked. And, they could still be.

Theirs remains an enduring call to action. So, can wearables create possibilities to act differently? And, what kinds of worlds might they make? Our response to these questions is informed not only by the breadth of the materials covered in *Wearable Utopias* but also in our orientation to the content. Drawing on STS, citizenship, gender, and cultural studies, we framed discussions around critical social and political issues and controversies such as menstruation, urban harassment, and pervasive surveillance. We set out to understand what wearables *do*, rather than focus on their visual appearance. There are many accounts of wearables that *do* something in this collection. Examples include wearables that provide the means to dress professionally for work and claim expert identities (see *Unhidden*), to relieve yourself safely and hygienically in public (see *Shewee*), or to respond to verbal abuse from other street users (see *Ride With Wolves*). Some projects create conditions for personal expression through designs that celebrate bodies, or body parts, that are often contained, shamed, or hidden (see *Body as Material, Iyá Àlàro*, and *Qué Rico Menstruo*). Wearables can provide a platform for debate and discussion about societal issues, such as air pollution and immigration (see *Catalytic Clothing* and *The Social Studio*). These examples—just a small selection from our research—demonstrate wearable evidence of how "citizenship is embodied and changed" via "new forms of togetherness" and "new strategies to claim rights and new civic roles."[3]

Our approach scrutinized the role of objects—things—in civic participation and public life. We explored if wearables could be understood as alternative "acts" and "performances" of citizenship. We have been guided by interdisciplinary scholars interested in how alternative forms of citizenship are made from the ground up, rather than through conventional, top-down, information-based relationships with the nation-state. We were motivated by political scholar Engin Isin's call for "a new vocabulary of citizenship" to reflect how "acts of citizenship stretch across boundaries, frontiers and territories to involve multiple and overlapping scales of contestation, belonging, identification and struggle."[4] Following sociologist Noortje Marres, we analyzed how people use objects and materials to creatively participate in civic life and organize political action on a daily and often mundane basis.[5] We have also sought what Bruno Latour describes in *Making Things Public* as an "object-oriented democracy" that embraces difference, builds individual and collective forms of expression, and "bind(s) us all in ways that map out a public space profoundly different from what is usually recognised under the label of 'the political.'"[6]

We also introduced this book with José Esteban Muñoz's invitation to refuse to settle for the status quo and his call for more vibrant, hopeful, and collective futures. The leading-edge designs in this collection provide an abundance of inspiration for the task. An example in practice is Sky Cubacub's concept of "radical visibility," which celebrates a diversity of bodies, genders, and abilities. Sky sees it as "a movement based on claiming our bodies," and it is through the innovative use of "bright colors, exuberant fabrics, and innovative designs" that they joyfully highlight and celebrate communities "that society typically shuns." This is just one of many interviews in this collection that surface "new sites of contestation, belonging, identification and struggle."[7]

Wearable Utopias unites these ideas through an examination of wearables. As outlined in the introduction, wearables touch every single body across the planet and are therefore ubiquitous in social, cultural, and political spheres. However, they are rarely considered central to an "object-oriented democracy." Ours remains a topic of enquiry more often found in fashion than in STS. Yet what we wear constitutes the "thingness" of wearable technoscience and powerfully informs the making, remaking, and reimagining of social and political worlds. We have shown how new forms of wearables worn in many contexts can enable individuals to "act as citizens" and "constitute themselves as those with the 'right to claim rights.'"[8]

The designers we interviewed do this in many ways. By grouping their diverse responses into six themes, we drew attention to the many creative methods through which challenging (often enduring) issues can be addressed. We hope this structure offers fresh perspectives on the sociopolitics of citizenship that expand beyond narrow, top-down, state-based relationships. Within each theme, the designers' approaches reorientate "problems" into sites of radical thinking and acting with, about, and in wearable form. They use wearables to mediate and translate between bodies, spaces, and politics in unexpected, unsettling, and vibrant ways, questioning and negotiating society in the process. In the process, they blur conventional understandings of singular, or fixed ideas of civic engagement.

These ideas map onto classic STS writings about the power of multiplicity, adaptability, and flexibility. In *The Body Multiple*, Annemarie Mol unsettles the idea of a thing, in this case a disease, as a stable or defined entity. She writes, "There is no longer a single passive object in the middle, waiting to be seen from the point of view of a seemingly endless series of perspectives."[9] Rather, she shows how different medical experts have multiple perspectives on one object—the body—yet cohesion is still possible. They don't have to compete or operate in a hierarchy. Multiple ideas can be assembled in different configurations to benefit different users. Far from weakening, here multiplicity can strengthen artifacts and systems. Building on this idea, citizenship studies scholar Sabine Netz and colleagues argue that "if bodies are multiple, they can be different, and other worlds are possible."[10]

Recognition and celebration of multiplicity is a key idea running through the collection. The designers do not smooth over or seek to erase difference. Rather, they highlight and expand—as well as move, conceal, connect, leak, and work—to embrace breadth and diversity as democratic alternatives to conventional norms. All are dedicated long-term members of, or work closely alongside, communities that are routinely overlooked, undervalued, or negatively targeted for being different. Drawing on distinctive, situated knowledges and experiences, they render visible a broader range of citizens who defy conventional understandings or binaries. The results make unexpected, ground-up and embodied interventions in everyday life. Fundamentally, they reveal the beauty and strength in difference.

Being seen matters on many levels. The designers don't just support people with appropriate, accessible, and imaginative wearables. Many also set out to transform sites of exclusion and marginalization into platforms for change. They provide tools for undoing and remaking norms and beliefs. Working in or closely with communities, they challenge taboos and provide critical reminders that what might be mundane for some can be isolating for others. As Rosemarie Garland-Thomson writes, "Although misfitting can lead to segregation, exclusion from the rights of citizenship, and alienation from a majority community, it can also foster intense awareness of social injustice and the formation of a community of misfits that can collaborate to achieve a more liberatory politics and praxis."[11] The power of the wearables in this collection lies in their ability to reveal hegemonic norms by opposing and subverting them.

These are some of the desire lines that pervade this book. They route across normative and dominant landscapes, making alternative tracks and traces and offering novel ways of navigating familiar journeys. We attempted to unite them, to highlight where they intersect, twist, and entwine with each other to explore how the expansive and imaginative offerings of these designers draw attention to the limitations and exclusions of normative sociopolitics. Rather than trying to speak for everyone, the wearables we have curated here respond to issues affecting specific groups and interstitial spaces that are often overlooked, ignored, or underrepresented. The work of the contributing designers showcase alternative possibilities for civic participation and political engagement and importantly remind us that change comes in a myriad of shapes, sizes, and speeds. It might be on show or cleverly concealed. It might ever so slightly nudge or subversively twist a conventional norm. It might capture the world's attention overnight, or acceptance might take an achingly long time . . . if it arrives at all. Regardless, these designers are committed to making new worlds, and they offer, as Carl DiSalvo writes, "a way to care, together, for our collective futures."[12]

Initializing a nascent desire line is difficult, for it involves heading into uncharted territory, veering away from the norm or separating from what is expected. In many ways, desire lines map onto Muñoz's writings about making and navigating new futures—or what he calls a "flight plan for a collective political becoming."[13] He invites readers "to look beyond a narrow version of the here and now" and insist "on something else, something better, something dawning." It is a hopeful provocation to step out of "this place and time to something fuller, vaster, more sensual, and brighter."[14] The world shouldn't only fit some citizens. Making and wearing things differently is one way we can reveal the systems of oppression, discrimination, and authority that structure and delimit many people's lives. Once we see and unsettle their hold over us, it becomes possible to imagine, invent, and inhabit new, more utopian worlds.

Notes

INTRODUCTION

1. Sarah Ahmed, *Queer Phenomenology: Orientations, Objects, Others* (Durham, NC: Duke University Press 2006), 19–20.

2. Robert Macfarlane, Twitter, @RobGMacfarlane, 7.00 am, March 25, 2018, https://twitter .com/robgmacfarlane/status/977787226133278725?lang=en.

3. Su Ballard, Joyce Zita, and Lizzie Muller, "Editorial Essay: Networked Utopias and Speculative Futures," *Faculty of Law, Humanities and the Arts*—Papers 380 (2012): 6.

4. Elizabeth Boneman, "What Are Desire Paths?" *Urban Geography, Geography Realm*, November 29, 2021, https://www.geographyrealm.com/what-are-desire-paths/.

5. José Esteban Muñoz, ed., *Cruising Utopia: The, Then and There of Queer Futurity* (New York: New York University Press, 2009), 1.

6. Diana Crane, *Fashion and its Social Agendas: Class, Gender and Identity in Clothing* (Chicago: University of Chicago Press 2000), 99.

7. Noortje Marres and Javier Lezaun, "Materials and Devices of the Public: An Introduction," *Economy and Society* 40, no. 4 (2011): 491.

8. Donna Haraway, *Staying with the Trouble: Making Kin in the Chthulucene* (Durham, NC: Duke University Press 2016), 12.

9. Bruno Latour, "From Realpolitik to Dingpolitik or How to Make Things Public," in *Making Things Public: Atmospheres of Democracy*, ed. Bruno Latour and Peter Weibel (Cambridge, MA: MIT Press, 2005), 15.

10. Daniel Miller, "Why Clothing is not Superficial," in *Stuff* (Cambridge: Polity Press, 2010), 23.

11. Shahidha Bari, *Dressed: The Secret Life of Clothes* (London: Penguin Random House, 2019), 10–11.

12. See Joanne Entwistle, "The Fashioned Body 15 Years On: Contemporary Fashion Thinking," *Fashion Practice* 8, no. 1 (2016): 15–21; Angela McRobbie, *Be Creative: Making a Living in the New Culture Industries* (Cambridge: Polity Press, 2016).

13. See Wiebe Bijker, *Of Bicycles, Bakelite, and Bulbs: Toward a Theory of Sociotechnical Change* (Cambridge, MA: MIT Press, 1997); Gay Hawkins, *The Ethics of Waste: How We Relate to Rubbish* (London: Rowman and Littlefield, 2006); Mike Michael, *Reconnecting Culture, Technology & Nature: From Society to Heterogeneity* (London: Routledge, 2012).

14. Susan Leigh Star, "The Ethnography of Infrastructure," *American Behavioural Scientist* 43, no. 3 (1999): 377–391.

15. Bruno Latour, "Where Are the Missing Masses? The Sociology of a Few Mundane Artifacts," in *Shaping Technology/Building Society: Studies in Sociotechnical Change*, ed. Wiebe Bijker and John Law (Cambridge, MA: MIT Press, 1994), 225–258.

16. Michael, *Reconnecting*, 4.

17. Rosemarie Garland-Thomson, "Misfits: A Feminist Materialist Disability Concept," *Hypatia* 26, no. 3 (Summer, 2011): 596.

18. Garland-Thomson, *Misfits*, 594, 595.

19. Garland-Thomson, *Misfits*, 594, 597.

20. Donna Haraway, "Situated Knowledges: The Science Question in Feminism and the Privilege of Partial Perspective," *Feminist Studies* 14, no. 3 (1988): 583.

21. Sara Ahmed, *What's the Use? On the Uses of Use* (Durham, NC: Duke University Press, 2019), 26.

22. Rosika Parker, *The Subversive Stitch: Embroidery and the Making of the Feminine* (London: Bloomsbury Visual Arts, 2012), ix.

23. For a detailed analysis of her work, see Stephanie DeGooyer, Alastair Hunt, Lida Maxwell, and Samuel Moyn, *The Right to Have Rights* (London: Verso, 2018).

24. Ruth Lister, *Citizenship: Feminist Perspectives*, 2nd ed. (New York: New York University Press, 2003), 2.

25. See Marie Sépulchre, *Disability and Citizenship Studies* (New York: Routledge, 2021); Beverley Skeggs, *Formations of Class and Gender* (London: Sage, 1997).

26. Sépulchre, *Disability and Citizenship Studies*, 1.

27. Paula Hildebrandt, Kerstin Evert, Sybille Peters, Mirjam Schaub, Kathrin Wildner, and Gesa Ziemer, eds, *Performing Citizenship: Bodies, Agencies, Limitations* (Cham: Palgrave Macmillan, 2019).

28. Engin Isin and Greg Neilson, eds., *Acts of Citizenship* (London: Zed Books 2008), 2.

29. Engin Isin, "Citizenship in Flux: The Figure of the Activist Citizen," *Subjectivity* 29 (2009): 371.

30. See, for example, Matt Ratto and Megan Boler, eds., *DIY Citizenship: Critical Making and Social Media* (Cambridge, MA: MIT Press, 2014); Jennifer Gabrys, "Citizen Sensing, Air Pollution and Fracking: From 'Caring about Your Air' to Speculative Practices of Evidencing Harm," *The Sociological Review* 65, no. 2 (2017):172–192; Kat Jungnickel. "Clothing Inventions as Acts of Citizenship? The Politics of Material Participation, Wearable Technologies,

and Women Patentees in Late Victorian Britain," *Science, Technology & Human Values* 48, no. 1 (2021): 9–33.

31. Paula Hildebrandt and Sybille Peters, "Introduction," 1–14, in *Performing Citizenship: Bodies, Agencies, Limitations*, ed. Paula Hildebrandt et al. (Cham: Palgrave Macmillan, 2019), 5.

32. Engin Isin, "Doing Rights with Things: The Art of Becoming Citizen," 45–56, in *Performing Citizenship: Bodies, Agencies, Limitations*, ed. Paula Hildebrandt et al. (Cham: Palgrave Macmillan, 2019), 51.

33. See http://www.PoliticsofPatents.org.

34. Noortje Marres, *Material Participation* (London: Palgrave Macmillan, 2015), 7.

35. Carl DiSalvo, *Design as Democratic Inquiry* (Cambridge, MA: MIT Press, 2022), 15.

36. Marres and Lezaun, *Materials*, 491–492.

37. Isin and Neilson, *Acts*, 4.

38. Netz et al., *Claiming*, 639.

39. Ahmed, *Queer*, 21.

CHAPTER 1

1. See International Alliance of Inhabitants, *World Charter for the Right to the City* (2005), https://www.uclg-cisdp.org/sites/default/files/documents/files/2021-06/WorldCharterRighttoCity.pdf; UNESCO, *International Public Debates: Urban Policies and the Right to the City* (Paris: UNESCO; UN-HABITAT 2006); *The Right to the City: Bridging the Urban Divide* (Rio de Janeiro: World Urban Forum, United Nations, 2010).

2. Garland-Thomson, *Misfits*, 601. See also Hannah Arendt, *The Human Condition*, 2nd ed. (Chicago: University of Chicago Press, 1998) and Jürgen Habermas, *The Structural Transformation of the Public Sphere: An Inquiry into a Category of Bourgeois Society* (Cambridge, MA: MIT Press, 1991).

3. Henri Lefebvre, *Le Droit á la Ville/The Right to the City* (Paris: Anthropos, 1968/1996).

4. Garland-Thomson, *Misfits*, 594.

5. Jane Darke, "The Man-Shaped City," in *Changing Places: Women's Lives in the City*, ed. Chris Booth, Jane Darke, and Sue Yeandle (London: Sage, 1996), 88.

6. See also Ursula Lutzky and Robert Lawson, "Gender Politics and Discourses of #mansplainng, #manspreading and #maninterruption on Twitter," *Social Media & Society* 5, no. 3 (2019): 1–12.

7. Leslie Kern, *Feminist City* (Toronto: Verso Books 2021), 149.

8. Doreen Massey, *Space, Place and Gender* (Cambridge, UK: Polity Press 1994), 185.

9. Nirmal Puwar, *Space Invaders: Race, Gender and Bodies Out of Place* (Oxford: Bloomsbury 2004), 8.

10. Megan Williams, "How City Planners Could Help Women Feel Safer," *CBC News*, October 7, 2014, https://www.cbc.ca/news/how-city-planners-could-help-women-feel-safer-1.2790046.

11. Hoda Katebi, "Op-Ed: Iranian Women Are Rising Up to Demand Freedom. Are We Listening?" *Los Angeles Times*, September 24, 2022, https://www.latimes.com/opinion/story/2022-09-24/iran-protests-mahsa-amini-hijab-morality-police.

12. Saurabh Sharma and Danish Siddiqui, "Protests Rumble in India Over Alleged Gang Rape of Young Woman," *Reuters*, October 2, 2020, https://www.reuters.com/article/us-india-rape-protests-idUSKBN26N22K.

13. Larry Buchanan, Quoctrung Bui, and Jugal K. Patel, "Black Lives Matter May Be the Largest Movement in U.S History," *New York Times*, July 3, 2020, https://www.nytimes.com/interactive/2020/07/03/us/george-floyd-protests-crowd-size.html.

14. Puwar, *Space*, 8.

15. See http://www.RebirthGarments.com

16. Chainmaille is a process involving opening and closing small metal rings with pliers in different weaves to create a textile or jewelry. Scalemaille uses small metal scales instead of rings.

17. Paulina Kieliba, Danielle Clode, Roni O, Maimon-Mor, and Tamar R. Makin, "Robotic Hand Augmentation Drives Changes in Neural Body Representation," *Science Robotics* 6, no. 54 (2021). https://doi.org/10.1126/scirobotics.abd79

CHAPTER 2

1. Pierre de Coubertin, "The Women at the Olympic Games," in *Pierre de Coubertin 1863–1937)—Olympism: Selected Writings*, ed. Norbert Müller (Lausanne: International Olympic Committee, 1912), 713.

2. Jennifer Hargreaves, *Heroines of Sport: The Politics of Difference and Identity* (London: Routledge 2000), 209.

3. Kat Jungnickel, "Convertible, Multiple, and Hidden: The Inventive Lives of Women's Sport and Activewear 1890–1940," *The Sociological Review*, First online March 2 (2023), 5.

4. Natasha Vertinsky, *The Eternally Wounded Woman: Women, Doctors and Exercise in the Late Nineteenth Century* (Urbana: University of Illinois Press 1994), 22.

5. Sport England, *Reframing Sport for Teenage Girls: Tackling Teenage Disengagement* (Women In Sport, 2022), https://www.womeninsport.org/wp-content/uploads/2022/03/Tackling-Teenage-Disengagement-March-2022.pdf.

6. Sport England, *Reframing*, 18.

7. See, for example, Katie Falkingham, "World Athletics Bans Transgender Women from Competing in Female World Ranking Events," *BBC Sport*, March 23, 2023, https://www.bbc.co.uk/sport/athletics/65051900.

8. Surf Life Saving Australia is a not-for-profit community organization that promotes water safety and life-saving. https://sls.com.au.

9. The Cronulla race riots were a series of violent protests in south Sydney in 2005 by 5,000 mostly Anglo-Australians "reclaiming the beach from outsiders." It exposed deep racial tensions and generated heated debates about multiculturalism in Australia. See https://www.nma.gov.au/defining-moments/resources/cronulla-race-riots.

10. Clarissa Pinkola Estés, *Women Who Run with the Wolves: Myths and Stories of the Wild Woman Archetype* (London: Rider, 1992).

CHAPTER 3

1. James Rule, "'Needs' for Surveillance and the Movement to Protect Privacy," in *Routledge Handbook of Surveillance Studies*, ed. Kirstie Ball, Kevin Haggerty, and David Lyon (New York: Routledge, 2012), 64.

2. David Lyon, *Surveillance Studies: An Overview* (Cambridge, UK: Polity Press, 2007).

3. Simone Browne, "Race and Surveillance," in *Routledge Handbook of Surveillance Studies*, ed. Kirstie Ball, Kevin Haggerty, and David Lyon (New York: Routledge, 2012), 72.

4. Rachel Dubrofsky and Shoshana Amielle Magnet, eds., *Feminist Surveillance Studies* (Durham, NC: Duke University Press, 2015), 3.

5. See the Universal Declaration of Human Rights (Article 12), the European Convention of Human Rights (Article 8). and the European Charter of Fundamental Rights (Article 7).

6. https://dictionary.cambridge.org/dictionary/english/conceal.

7. Bari, *Dressed*, 13.

8. Barbara Burman and Ariane Fennetaux, *The Pocket: A Hidden History of Women's Lives, 1660-1900* (New Haven, CT: Yale University Press, 2019).

9. John Gilliom and Torin Monahan, "Everyday Resistance," in *Routledge Handbook of Surveillance Studies*, ed. Kirstie Ball, Kevin Haggerty, and David Lyon (New York: Routledge, 2012), 410.

CHAPTER 4

1. Crane, *Fashion*, 100.

2. Wendy Parkins, "'The Epidemic of Purple, White and Green': Fashion and the Suffragette Movement in Britain 1908–14." In Fashioning the Body Politic, edited by Wendy Parkins. Oxford: Berg Publishers, 2002), 99.

3. Lisa Tickner, *The Spectacle of Women: Imagery of the Suffrage Campaign 1907–14* (London: Chatto & Windus 1987), ix.

4. January 26 marks the starts of the colonization of Australia by British forces in 1788.

5. See Clothingthegaps.com.au.

6. Eleanor Johnson and Håvard Haarstad, "Competing Climate Spectacles in the Amplified Public Space," *Environment and Planning C: Politics and Space* 40, no. 7 (2022): 1438.

7. Bari, *Dressed*, 9–10.

8. Wendy Parkins, ed., *Fashioning the Body Politic* (Oxford: Berg Publishers 2002), 2.

9. Crane, *Fashion*, 3.

10. Liz Reich, "Performing Citizenship: Gathering (in the) Movement," in *Performing Citizenship*, ed. Hildebrandt et al. (Cham: Palgrave Macmillan 2019), 57.

11. Donna Haraway, "A Game of Cat's Cradle: Science Studies, Feminist Theory, Cultural Studies," *Configurations* 2, no. 1 (1994): 3.

12. Krista Suh, *DIY Rules for a WTF World: How to Speak Up, Get Creative and Change the World* (New York: Grand Central Publishing, 2018).

13. A Catalytic Converter in a motorized vehicle converts toxic gases and pollutants from exhaust gas into less toxic pollutants.

14. Nanosized particles of titanium dioxide.

15. See https://www.reconciliation.org.au/blak-black-blackfulla-language-is-important-but-it-can-be-tricky/.

16. Kangas are bright, colorful printed (mostly) cotton fabric often worn by women as a skirt, head-wrap, or apron.

CHAPTER 5

1. Natasha Preskey, "Coronavirus Lockdown Has Shown That Access to Public Loos Is More Vital Than Ever," *INews*, July 13, 2020, https://inews.co.uk/opinion/public-toilets-uk-coronavirus-lockdown-433507.

2. Ritwika Mitra, "100 Women: How the 'Urinary Leash' Keeps Women at Home," *BBC News*, November 19, 2017, https://www.bbc.com/news/world-41999792.

3. See, for example, Elizabeth Grosz, *Volatile Bodies: Toward a Corporeal Feminism* (Bloomington: Indiana University Press 1994); Robyn Longhurst, *Bodies: Exploring Fluid Boundaries* (London: Routledge 2001).

4. Mary Douglas, *Purity and Danger: An Analysis of Concepts of Pollution and Taboo* (Oxon, UK: Routledge, 1966).

5. Longhurst, *Bodies*, 2; Margaret Shildrick, *Leaky Bodies and Boundaries: Feminism, Postmodernism and (Bio)ethics* (London: Routledge, 1997).

6. Natalie Moffat and Lucy Pickering, "'Out of Order': The Double Burden of Menstrual Etiquette and the Subtle Exclusion of Women from Public Space in Scotland," *The Sociological Review Monographs* 67, no. 4 (2019): 766–787.

7. Moffat and Pickering, "'Out of Order,'" 767.

8. Grosz, *Volatile*, 206.

9. Phillippa Wiseman, "Lifting the Lid: Disabled Toilets as Sites of Belonging and Embodied Citizenship," *The Sociological Review Monographs* 67, no. 4 (2019): 789.

10. Wiseman, *Lifting*, 789.

11. Jack Halberstam, *Female Masculinity* (Durham, NC: Duke University Press, 2018), 22, 24.

12. Halberstam, *Female*, 22.

13. Alexander David, *Bathroom Battle Grounds: How Public Restrooms Shape the Gender Order* (Oakland: University of California Press, 2020).

14. Sheila Cavanagh, *Queering Bathrooms: Gender, Sexuality and the Hygienic Imagination* (Toronto: University of Toronto Press 2011), 5.

15. Sarita Vijay Panchang, "Women 'Holding It' in Urban India: Toilet Avoidance as an Under-Recognized Health Outcome of Sanitation Insecurity," *Global Public Health* 17, no. 4 (2020):587-600.

16. Nioshi Shah, "The Right to Pee: The Gender and Caste Privileges of Urination," *Feminism India*, April 10, 2020, https://feminisminindia.com/2020/04/10/right-to-pee-gender-caste-privileges-urination.

17. Shilpa Phadke, *Why Loiter? Women and Risk on Mumbai Streets* (New Delhi: Penguin Books, 2011).

18. Adam Eldridge, "Public Panics: Problem Bodies in Social Space," *Emotion, Space and Society* 3 (2010): 41.

19. Eldridge, *Public*, 42.

20. Clara Greed, *Inclusive Urban Design: Public Toilets* (London: Elsevier, Architectural Press, 2003), 6.

21. Wiseman, *Lifting*, 790.

22. The James Dyson Award is an annual international competition for new inventors that "celebrates, encourages and inspires the next generation of design engineers." See https://www.jamesdysonaward.org.

23. Caroline Criado Perez, *Invisible Women: Exposing Data Bias in a World Designed for Men* (London: Vintage, 2020).

24. Trade Union Congress Report, "Personal Protective Equipment and Women: Guidance for Workplace Representatives on Ensuring It Is a Safe Fit," April 25, 2017, https://www.tuc.org.uk/sites/default/files/PPEandwomenguidance.pdf.

CHAPTER 6

1. Trade Union Congress Report, "New Analysis Shows Pay Gap between Non-Disabled and Disabled Workers Is Now 17.2%, or £3,700 a Year," November 7, 2022, https://www.tuc.org.uk/news/non-disabled-workers-paid-17-more-disabled-peers-tuc.

2. Merja Tarvainen and Vilma Hänninen, "Disability and Working-Life Citizenship," *Nordic Social Work Research* 13, no. 3 (2022): 469.

3. Sangkyung Bae and Moon Choi, "Age and Workplace Ageism: A Systematic Review and Meta-Analysis," *Journal of Gerontological Social Work* 66, no. 6 (2023): 724–738.

4. Diva Dhar, "Women's Unpaid Care Work Has Been Unmeasured and Undervalued for Too Long," *Global Institute for Women's Leadership's new Essays on Equality* (London: Kings College, 2020).

5. Carolina Aragão, "Gender Pay Gap in U.S Hasn't Changed Much in Two Decades," *Pew Research Centre*, March 1, 2023, https://www.pewresearch.org/fact-tank/2023/03/01/gender-pay-gap-facts.

6. Judy Wajcman, *Feminism Confronts Technology* (Philadelphia: Pennsylvania State University Press, 1991); Judy Wajcman, *Technofeminism* (Cambridge, UK: Polity Press 2004); Cynthia Cockburn and Susan Ormrod, *Gender and Technology in the Making* (London: Sage 1994); Ruth Schwartz-Cowan, *More Work for Mother: The Ironies of Household Technology From the Open Hearth to the Microwave* (New York: Basic Books, 1985).

7. Susan Leigh Star and Anslem Strauss, "Layers of Silence, Arenas of Voice: The Ecology of Visible and Invisible Work," *Computer Supported Cooperative Work* 8, no. 1 (1999): 10.

8. Star and Strauss, "Layers of Silence."

9. Wajcman, *Technofeminism*, 41.

10. Schwartz-Cowan, *More Work for Mother, 3*.

11. Sara Berg, "Ill-Fitting PPE Contributes to Added Stress for Women Physicians," *American Medical Association*, September 1, 2021, https://www.ama-assn.org/delivering-care/public-health/ill-fitting-ppe-contributes-added-stress-women-physicians; Zoe Kleinman, "PPE 'Designed for Women' Needed on Frontline," *BBC News*, April 29, 2020, https://www.bbc.co.uk/news/health-52454741.

12. Aimi Hamraie and Kelly Fritsch, "Crip Technoscience Manifesto," *Catalyst: Feminism, Theory, Technoscience* 5, no. 1 (2019): 5–6.

13. Garland-Thomson, *Misfits*, 603.

14. Daggy is Australian slang for unfashionable or not stylish.

15. Ari Seth Cohen, *Advanced Style* (New York: Powerhouse Books, 2012).

CHAPTER 7

1. Wiebe Bijker and John Law, *Shaping Technology/Building Society: Studies in Sociotechnical Change* (Cambridge, MA: MIT Press, 1992), 3.

2. Bijker and Law, *Shaping*, 3

3. Hildebrandt and Peters, *Introduction*, 1.

4. Isin, *Citizenship in Flux*, 368, 371.

5. Marres, *Material*, 7.

6. Latour, *Realpolitik*, 15.

7. Isin, *Citizenship in Flux*, 371.

8. Isin, *Citizenship in Flux*, 371.

9. Annemarie Mol, *The Body Multiple: Ontology in Medical Practice* (Durham, NC: Duke University Press, 2002), 5.

10. Sabine Netz et al., "Claiming Citizenship Rights through the Body Multiple," *Citizenship Studies* 23, no. 7 (2019): 646.

11. Garland-Thomson, *Misfits*, 598.

12. DiSalvo, *Design*, 2.

13. Muñoz, *Cruising*, 189.

14. Muñoz, *Cruising*, 189.

References

Ahmed, Sara. *What's The Use? On the uses of use,* Durham, NC: Duke University Press, 2019.

Ahmed, Sara. *Queer Phenomenology.* Durham, NC: Duke University Press, 2006.

Aragão, Carolina. "Gender Pay Gap in U.S. Hasn't Changed Much in Two Decades." *Pew Research Centre,* March 1, 2023. https://www.pewresearch.org/fact-tank/2023/03/01/gender-pay-gap-facts/.

Arendt, Hannah. *The Human Condition,* 2nd ed. (Chicago: University of Chicago Press, 1998).

Bae, Sangkyung, and Moon Choi. "Age and Workplace Ageism: A Systematic Review and Meta-Analysis," *Journal of Gerontological Social Work* 66, no. 6 (2023): 724–738.

Ballard, Su, Joyce Zita, and Lizzie Muller. "Editorial Essay: Networked Utopias and Speculative Futures." *Faculty of Law, Humanities and the Arts—Papers* 380 (2012): 6.

Bari, Shahidha. *Dressed: The Secret Life of Clothes.* London: Penguin Random House, 2019.

Berg, Sara. "Ill-Fitting PPE Contributes to Added Stress for Women Physicians." *American Medical Association,* September 1, 2021. https://www.ama-assn.org/delivering-care/public-health/ill-fitting-ppe-contributes-added-stress-women-physicians.

Bijker, Wiebe. *Of Bicycles, Bakelites, and Bulbs: Toward a Theory of Sociotechnical Change.* Cambridge, MA: MIT Press, 1997.

Bijker, Wiebe, and John Law. *Shaping Technology/Building Society: Studies in Sociotechnical Change.* Cambridge, MA: MIT Press, 1992.

Boneman, Elizabeth. "What Are Desire Paths?" *Urban Geography, Geography Realm,* November 29, 2021. https://www.geographyrealm.com/what-are-desire-paths/.

Browne, Simone. "Race and Surveillance." In *Routledge Handbook of Surveillance Studies,* edited by Kirstie Ball, Kevin Haggerty, and David Lyon, 72–79. New York: Routledge, 2012.

Buchanan, Larry, Quoctrung Bui, and Jugal K. Patel. "Black Lives Matter May Be the Largest Movement in U.S History." *New York Times,* July 3, 2020. https://www.nytimes.com/interactive/2020/07/03/us/george-floyd-protests-crowd-size.html.

Burman, Barbara, and Ariane Fennetaux. *The Pocket: A Hidden History of Women's Lives, 1660–1900.* New Haven, CT: Yale University Press, 2019.

Cavanagh, Sheila. *Queering Bathrooms: Gender, Sexuality and the Hygienic Imagination*. Toronto: University of Toronto Press, 2011.

Crane, Diana. *Fashion and Its Social Agenda: Class, Gender and Identity in Clothing*. Chicago: University of Chicago Press, 2000.

Criado Perez, Caroline. *Invisible Women: Exposing Data Bias in a World Designed for Men*. London: Chatto & Windus, 2019.

Cockburn, Cynthia, and Susan Ormrod. *Gender and Technology in the Making*. London: Sage, 1994.

Cohen, Ari Seth. *Advanced Style*. New York: Powerhouse Books, 2012.

Darke, Jane. "The Man-Shaped City." In *Changing Places: Women's Lives in the City*, edited by Chris Booth, Jane Darke, and Sue Yeandle. London: Sage, 1996.

David, Alexander. *Bathroom Battle Grounds: How Public Restrooms Shape the Gender Order*. Oakland: University of California Press, 2020.

de Coubertin, Pierre. "The Women at the Olympic Games." In *Pierre de Coubertin 1863-1937)—Olympism: Selected Writings*, edited by Norbert Müller, 713. Lausanne: International Olympic Committee, 1912.

DeGooyer, Stephanie, Alastair Hunt, Lida Maxwell, and Samuel Moyn. *The Right to Have Rights*. London: Verso, 2018.

Dhar, Diva. "Women's Unpaid Care Work Has Been Unmeasured and Undervalued for Too Long." In *Essays on Equality*, edited by Global Institute for Women's Leadership, 30–33. London: Kings College, 2019.

DiSalvo, Carl. *Design as Democratic Inquiry*. Cambridge MA: MIT Press, 2022.

Douglas, Mary. *Purity and Danger: An Analysis of Concepts of Pollution and Taboo*. London: Routledge, 1966.

Dubrofsky, Rachel E., and Shoshana A. Magnet. *Feminist Surveillance Studies*. Durham, NC: Duke University Press, 2015.

Eldridge, Adam. "Public Panics: Problem Bodies in Social Space." *Emotion, Space and Society* 3 (2010): 40–44.

Entwistle, Joanne. "The Fashioned Body 15 Years On: Contemporary Fashion Thinking." *Fashion Practice* 8, no. 1 (2016): 15–21.

Falkingham, Katie. "World Athletics Bans Transgender Women from Competing in Female World Ranking Events." *BBC Sport*, March 23, 2023. https://www.bbc.co.uk/sport/athletics/65051900

Fisher, Mark. *Capitalist Realism: Is There No Alternative?* Winchester: Zer0 Books, 2012.

Gabrys, Jennifer. "Citizen Sensing, 'Air Pollution and Fracking: From Caring about Your Air' to Speculative Practices of Evidencing Harm.'" *The Sociological Review* 65, no. 2 (2017): 172–192.

Garland-Thomson, Rosemarie. "Misfits: A Feminist Materialist Disability Concept." *Hypatia* 26, no. 3 (Summer, 2011): 591–609.

Gilliom, John, and Torin Monahan. "Everyday Resistance." In *Routledge Handbook of Surveillance Studies*, edited by Kirstie Ball, Kevin Haggerty, and David Lyon, 405–411. New York: Routledge, 2012.

Greed, Clara. *Inclusive Urban Design: Public Toilets*. Oxford: Elsevier, Architectural Press, 2003.

Grosz, Elizabeth. *Volatile Bodies: Toward a Corporeal Feminism*. Bloomington: Indiana University Press, 1994.

Habermas, Jürgen. *The Structural Trans-formation of the Public Sphere: An Inquiry into a Category of Bourgeois Society* (Cambridge, MA: MIT Press, 1991).

Halberstam, Jack. *Female Masculinity*. Durham, NC: Duke University Press, 2018.

Haggerty, Kevin, and Richard Ericson. "The Surveillant Assemblage." *The British Journal of Sociology* 51, no. 4 (2000): 606.

Hamraie, Aimi, and Kelly Fritsch. "Crip Technoscience Manifesto." *Catalyst: Feminism, Theory, Technoscience* 5, no. 1 (2019): 1–34.

Hargreaves, Jennifer. *Heroines of Sport: The Politics of Difference and Identity*. London: Routledge, 2000.

Haraway, Donna. "Situated Knowledges: The Science Question in Feminism and the Privilege of Partial Perspective." *Feminist Studies* 14, no. 3 (1988): 575–599.

Haraway, Donna. "A Game of Cat's Cradle: Science Studies, Feminist Theory, Cultural Studies." *Configurations* 2, no. 1 (1994): 59–71.

Haraway, Donna. *Staying with the Trouble: Making Kin in the Chthulucene*. Durham, NC: Duke University Press 2016.

Hawkins, Gay. *The Ethics of Waste: How We Relate to Rubbish*. London: Rowman and Littlefield, 2006.

Hildebrandt, Paula, Kerstin Evert, Sybille Peters, Mirjam Schaub, Kathrin Wildner, and Gesa Ziemer, eds. *Performing Citizenship: Bodies, Agencies, Limitations*. Cham: Palgrave Macmillan, 2019.

Hildebrandt, Paula, and Sybille Peters. "Introduction." In *Performing Citizenship: Bodies, Agencies, Limitations*, edited by Paula Hildebrant et al., 1–14. Cham: Palgrave Macmillan, 2019.

Isin, Engin. "Doing Rights with Things: The Art of Becoming Citizen." In *Performing Citizenship: Bodies, Agencies, Limitations*, edited by Paula Hildebrandt et al., 45–56. Cham: Palgrave Macmillan, 2019.

Isin, Engin. "Citizenship in Flux: The Figure of the Activist Citizen." *Subjectivity* 29 (2009): 367–388.

Isin, Engen, and Greg Neilson, eds. *Acts of Citizenship*. London: Zed Books, 2008.

Johnson, Eleanor, and Håvard Haarstad. "Competing Climate Spectacles in the Amplified Public Space." *Environment and Planning C: Politics and Space* 40, no. 7 (2022): 1403–1605.

Jungnickel, Kat. "Convertible, Multiple, and Hidden: The Inventive Lives of Women's Sport & Activewear 1890–1940." *The Sociological Review*, First online March 2 (2023): 1–23.

Jungnickel, Kat. "Clothing Inventions as Acts of Citizenship? The Politics of Material Participation, Wearable Technologies, and Women Patentees in Late Victorian Britain." *Science, Technology & Human Values* 48, no. 1 (2023): 9–33.

Katebi, Hoda. "Op-Ed: Iranian Women Are Rising Up to Demand Freedom. Are We Listening?" *Los Angeles Times*, September 24, 2022. https://www.latimes.com/opinion/story/2022-09-24/iran -protests-mahsa-amini-hijab-morality-police.

Kern, Leslie. *Feminist City.* London: Verso, 2020.

Kieliba, Paulina, Danielle Clode, Roni O, Maimon-Mor, and Tamar R. Makin. "Robotic Hand Augmentation Drives Changes in Neural Body Representation," *Science Robotics* 6, no. 54 (2021). https://doi.org/10.1126/scirobotics.abd79

Kleinman, Zoe. "PPE 'Designed for Women' Needed on Frontline." *BBC News*, April 29, 2020. https://www.bbc.co.uk/news/health-52454741.

Latour, Bruno. "Where Are the Missing Masses? The Sociology of a Few Mundane Artifacts." In *Shaping Technology/Building Society: Studies in Sociotechnical Change*, edited by Wiebe Bijker and John Law, 225–258. Cambridge, MA: MIT Press, 1994.

Latour, Bruno, and Peter Weibel, eds. *Making Things Public: Atmospheres of Democracy*. Cambridge, MA: MIT Press, 2005.

Lefebvre, Henri. *Le Droit á la Ville/The Right to the City*. Paris: Ellipses, 1968/1996.

Lister, Ruth. *Citizenship: Feminist Perspectives*. 2nd ed. New York: New York University Press, 2003.

Longhurst, Robyn. *Bodies: Exploring Fluid Boundaries*. London: Routledge, 2001.

Lutzky, Ursula, and Robert Lawson. "Gender Politics and Discourses of #mansplainng, #manspreading and #maninterruption on Twitter." *Social Media & Society* 5, no. 3 (2019): 1–12.

Lyon, David. *Surveillance Studies: An Overview*. Cambridge: Polity Press, 2007.

Macfarlane, Robert. Twitter, @RobGMacfarlane, 7.00 am, March 25, 2018, https://twitter.com /robgmacfarlane/status/977787226133278725?lang=en.

Marres, Noortje. *Material Participation*. London: Palgrave Macmillan, 2015.

Marres, Noortje, and Javier Lezaun. "Materials and Devices of the Public: An Introduction." *Economy and Society* 40, no. 4 (2011): 489–509.

Massey, Doreen. *Space, Place and Gender* (Cambridge, UK: Polity Press 1994).

McRobbie, Angela. *Be Creative: Making a Living in the New Culture Industries*. Cambridge: Polity Press, 2016.

Michael, Mike. *Reconnecting Culture, Technology & Nature: From Society to Heterogeneity*. London: Routledge, 2012.

Miller, Daniel. *Stuff*. Cambridge: Polity Press, 2010.

Mitra, Ritwika. "100 Women: How the 'Urinary Leash' Keeps Women at Home." *BBC News*, November 19, 2017. https://www.bbc.com/news/world-41999792

Moffat, Natalie, and Lucy Pickering. "'Out of Order': The Double Burden of Menstrual Etiquette and the Subtle Exclusion of Women from Public Space in Scotland." *The Sociological Review Monographs* 67, no. 4 (2019): 766–787.

Mol, Annemarie. *The Body Multiple: Ontology in Medical Practice.* Durham, NC: Duke University Press, 2002.

Muñoz, José Esteban, ed. *Cruising Utopia: The, Then and There of Queer Futurity.* New York: New York University Press, 2009.

Netz, Sabine, Sarah Lempp, Kristine Krause, and Schramm Katharina. "Claiming Citizenship Rights through the Body Multiple." *Citizenship Studies* 23, no. 7 (2019): 637–651.

Parker, Rosika. *The Subversive Stitch: Embroidery and the Making of the Feminine.* London: Bloomsbury Visual Arts, 2012.

Parkins, Wendy. "'The Epidemic of Purple, White and Green': Fashion and the Suffragette Movement in Britain 1908–14." In *Fashioning the Body Politic*, edited by Wendy Parkins. Oxford: Berg Publishers, 2002.

Phadke, Shilpa. *Why Loiter? Women And Risk on Mumbai Streets.* New Delhi: Penguin Books, 2011.

Pinkola Estés, Clarissa. *Women Who Run with the Wolves: Myths and Stories of the Wild Woman Archetype* (London: Rider, 1992).

Preskey, Natasha. "Coronavirus Lockdown Has Shown That Access to Public Loos Is More Vital Than Ever." *INews*, July 13, 2020. https://inews.co.uk/opinion/public-toilets-uk-coronavirus-lockdown-433507.

Puwar, Nirmal. *Space Invaders: Race, Gender and Bodies Out of Place* (Oxford: Bloomsbury 2004).

Ratto, Matt, and Megan Boler, eds. *DIY Citizenship: Critical Making and Social Media.* Cambridge, MA: MIT Press, 2014.

Rule, James. "'Needs' for Surveillance and the Movement to Protect Privacy." In *Routledge Handbook of Surveillance Studies*, edited by Kirstie Ball, Kevin Haggerty, and David Lyon, 64–71. New York: Routledge, 2012.

Schwartz-Cowan, Ruth. *More Work for Mother: The Ironies of Household Technology from the Open Hearth to the Microwave.* New York: Basic Books, 1983.

Sépulchre, Marie. *Disability and Citizenship Studies.* New York: Routledge, 2021.

Shah, Nioshi. "The Right to Pee: The Gender and Caste Privileges of Urination." *Feminism India*, 10 (2011). https://feminisminindia.com/2020/04/10/right-to-pee-gender-caste-privileges-urination/.

Sharma, Saurabh, and Danish Siddiqui. "Protests Rumble in India Over Alleged Gang Rape of Young Woman." *Reuters*, October 2, 2020. https://www.reuters.com/article/us-india-rape-protests-idUSKBN26N22K.

Shildrick, Margaret. *Leaky Bodies and Boundaries: Feminism, Postmodernism and (Bio)ethics.* London: Routledge, 1997.

Siwach, Prerna. "Mapping Gendered Spaces and Women's Mobility: A Case Study of Mitathal Village, Haryana." The Oriental Anthropologist 20, no. 1 (2020): 33–48.

Skeggs, Beverley. *Formations of Class and Gender*. London: Sage, 1997.

Sport England. *Reframing Sport for Teenage Girls: Tackling Teenage Disengagement*. Women In Sport, 2022. https://www.womeninsport.org/wp-content/uploads/2022/03/Tackling-Teenage-Disengagement-March-2022.pdf.

Star, Susan Leigh. "The Ethnography of Infrastructure." *American Behavioural Scientist* 43, no. 3 (1999): 377–391.

Star, Susan Leigh, and Anslem Strauss. "Layers of Silence, Arenas of Voice: The Ecology of Visible and Invisible Work." *Computer Supported Cooperative Work* 8, no. 1 (1999): 9–30.

Suh, Krista. *DIY Rules for a WTF World: How to Speak Up, Get Creative and Change the World* (New York: Grand Central Publishing, 2018).

Tarvainen, Merja, and Vilma Hänninen. "Disability and Working-Life Citizenship." *Nordic Social Work Research* 13, no. 3 (2022): 460–471. https://doi.org/10.1080/2156857X.2022.2032810.

Taylor, Harry. "One Arrested amid Tate Britain Protest Over Drag Queen Children's Event." *Guardian Online*, February 11, 2023. https://www.theguardian.com/world/2023/feb/11/tate-britain-protest-drag-queen-childrens-storytelling-event-arrest.

Tickner, Lisa. *The Spectacle of Women: Imagery of the Suffrage Campaign 1907-14*. London: Chatto and Windus, 1987.

Trade Union Congress. "New Analysis Shows Pay Gap between Non-Disabled and Disabled Workers Is Now 17.2%, or £3,700 a Year," November 7, 2022, https://www.tuc.org.uk/news/non-disabled-workers-paid-17-more-disabled-peers-tuc.

Trade Union Congress. "Personal Protective Equipment and Women: Guidance for Workplace Representatives on Ensuring It Is a Safe Fit," April 25, 2017, https://www.tuc.org.uk/sites/default/files/PPEandwomenguidance.pdf.

Vertinsky, Patricia. *The Eternally Wounded Woman. Women, Doctors, and Exercise in the Late Nineteenth Century*. Urbana: University of Illinois Press, 1994.

Vijay Panchang, Sarita. "Women 'Holding It' in Urban India: Toilet Avoidance as an Under-Recognized Health Outcome of Sanitation Insecurity." *Global Public Health* 17, no. 4 (2020): 587–600.

Wajcman, Judy. *Feminism Confronts Technology*. Philadelphia: Pennsylvania State University Press, 1991.

Wajcman, Judy. *Technofeminism*. Cambridge, UK: Polity Press, 2004.

Weber, Rachel. "Manufacturing Gender in Military Cockpit Design." In *The Social Shaping of Technology*, 2nd ed., edited by Donald Mackenzie and Judy Wajcman. Buckingham: Open University Press, 1999.

Williams, Megan. "How City Planners Could Help Women Feel Safer." *CBC News*, October 7, 2014. https://www.cbc.ca/news/how-city-planners-could-help-women-feel-safer-1.2790046.

Wiseman, Phillippa. "Lifting the Lid: Disabled Toilets as Sites of Belonging and Embodied Citizenship." *The Sociological Review Monographs* 67, no. 4 (2019): 788–806.

Index